PAGANISM

VIVIANNE CROWLEY

The publishers would like to thank Jillie Collings for her suggestion for the title of this series, *Principles of...*

Thorsons
An Imprint of HarperCollins*Publishers*
77–85 Fulham Palace Road,
Hammersmith, London W6 8JB
1160 Battery Sreet
San Francisco, California 94111–1213

Published by Thorsons 1996
9 10 8

A catalogue record for this book is available from the British Library

ISBN 0 85538 507 4

Text illustrations by Tony Meadows

Printed and bound in Great Britain by
Caledonian International Book Manufacturing Ltd, Glasgow, G64

PAGANISM

IN THE SAME SERIES:

Principles of Aromatherapy
Cathy Hopkins

Principles of Buddhism
Kulananda

Principles of Colonic Irrigation
Jillie Collings

Principles of the Enneagram
Karen Webb

Principles of Hypnotherapy
Vera Peiffer

Principles of NLP
Joseph O'Connor and Ian McDermott

Principles of Nutritional Therapy
Linda Lazarides

Principles of Self-Healing
David Lawson

Principles of Tarot
Evelyne and Terry Donaldson

TO THOSE WHO WALK THE ANCIENT PATHWAYS:
THE BLESSINGS OF EARTH AND SKY,
OF MOON AND SUN.

CONTENTS

THE RETURN OF THE GODS

Like a white bird upon the wind,
the sail of the boat of Manannán mac Lir,[1] the Son of the Sea,
flew across the sparkling waves
filled with the breeze that blew Westward to the Islands of the Blessed.
The Sun Goddess above him
smiled down with warmth upon her friend.
The fish in the ocean danced for him beneath the turquoise water;
the porpoises leapt above the waves to greet him.
Upon the wind was a smell of sweetness,
the smell of apple blossom in the Spring of the morning of the world.
And in the prow of the boat sat Lugh[2] the long-armed;
strumming on his harp, he sang the Song of Creation.
And as they drew closer to the green hills of Ireland, the holy land of Ireland,
the Shee came out of their earth-barrow homes
and danced for joy beneath the Sun.
For hidden in a crane-skin sack at the bottom of the boat
was the Holy Cup of Blessedness.
Long had been her journeying through lands strange and far.
And all who drank of that Cup,
dreamed the dreams of holy truth,
and drank of the Wine of everlasting life.
And deep within the woods,
in a green-clad clearing,
where the purple anemone and the white campion bloomed,
where primroses still lingered on the shadowed Northern side,
a great stag lifted up his antlered head and sniffed the morning.
His antlers seven-forked spoke of mighty battles fought and won,
red was his coat, the colour of fire,
and he trotted out of his greenwood home,

hearing on the wind the song of Lugh.
And in her deep barrow home,
the green clad Goddess of Erin,
remembered the tongue that she had forgotten.
She remembered the secrets of the weaving of spells,
She remembered the tides of woman
and the ebb and flow of wave and Moon.
She remembered the people who had turned to other Gods
and coming out of her barrow of sleep,
her sweet voice echoed the verses of Lugh and the chorus of
Manannán.
And the great stag of the morning came across the fields to her
and where had stood the Goddess now stood a white hind.
And the love of the God was returned by the Goddess
and the larks of Anghus mac Og hovering above the field
echoed with ecstasy the Song of Creation.
And in the villages and towns
the people came out of their houses,
hearing the sweet singing and seeking its source.
And children danced in the streets with delight.
And they went down to the shore, the Eastern shore,
where rises the Sun of the Morning,
and awaited the coming of Manannán and Lugh,
the mast of their boat shining gold in the Sun.
The sea had spoken,
the Eastern dawn had given up her secret,
the Gods were returning,
the Old Ones awakening,
joy was returning unto the sleeping land.

[1] Pronounced *Mananarn mak Leer*.
[2] Pronounced *Loo*.

PAGANISM TODAY

We are the heirs and propagators of Paganism...
Happy is he who, for the sake of Paganism,
bears the burdens of persecution with firm hope.
Who else have civilized the world,
and built the cities,
if not the nobles and kings of Paganism?
Who else have set in order the harbours and the rivers?
And who else have taught the hidden wisdom?
To who else has the Deity revealed itself,
given oracles, and told about the future,
if not to the famous men among the Pagans?
The Pagans have made known all this.
They have discovered the art of healing the soul;
they have also made known the art of healing the body.
They have filled the Earth with settled forms of government,
and with wisdom, which is the highest good.
Without Paganism the world would be empty and miserable.

THABIT IBN QURRA OF HARRAN, NINTH-CENTURY SAGE
QUOTED IN SCOTT, WALTER, ED., *Hermetica: The Ancient Greek and Latin Writings which contain Religious or Philosophic Teachings ascribed to Hermes Trismegistus*, VOL. I, SHAMBALA, BOSTON, 1985, P.105.

Paganism is one of the fastest growing spiritual movements in the West today. Pagans are those who worship the ancient pre-Christian Gods of our ancestors and of our lands. Originally, the word 'Pagan' was applied to those who worshipped the Gods of the *pagus*, which in Latin means 'locality'. Pagan was also used in another sense by Christians – to mean 'country-dweller'. 'Heathen', of German origin, is also used by those who worship the Northern European Gods. Heathen means the someone of the heath who worships the Gods of the land. 'Paganism' is not a word that our ancestors would have used and it is seen by some as derogatory. Outside Europe, Pagans often reject it as an example of Western colonialism denigrating their traditional beliefs. In West Africa, the followers of indigenous spirituality refer to their beliefs as African Traditional Religion. In the West, the terms Native Spirituality, Celtic Spirituality, European Traditional Religion, the Elder Faith and the Old Religion are also used to describe the Pagan religions.

PAGANS TODAY

To worship ancient deities may seem strange in our modern world. Why do Pagans worship these ancient and dusty images? We worship our Gods because they are not forgotten archaeological artefacts but living energies of great power. They have endured in their external images, their statues rescued from temples of long ago which now reside in museums all over the world, seated in temples of learning rather than of religion. More importantly, they have endured in the group memory of humanity, the collective unconscious, which is the storehouse of all our religious longing and experience.

Pagan religion is based on teachings handed down through myth and saga over thousands of years. Paganism has never died. Instead our ancient Pagan beliefs have been seen as merely myth or fairy stories, tales we learn at our mother's knee or in school, which have no relevance today. However, the fact that we cherish and pass on these myths shows that they do have relevance. Through generations and generations these tales have been passed down by word of mouth. They were sung to the Greek lyre across the waters of the sparkling Aegean Sea, caroused by Norwegian bards or skalds to their mead-drinking lords around smoking moot hall fires and spun from the mouths of silver-tongued Irish bards so revered that they were immune from all violence and harm and could walk the fiercest battlefield with impunity.

The myths have survived because they speak to us in the language of the night, the language of dream, symbol and allegory. They tease the conscious mind because we do not fully understand them; yet we know beneath their symbolism are undying truths. They are like grit in the shell of the oyster. Our minds work away at them, often outside our conscious awareness. They linger and remain when other tales are forgotten. They are retold in novels of fantasy and science fiction that sell in their millions. And, like the grit in the shell of the oyster, eventually they make a pearl of great price – the pearl of wisdom.

Myths are important because they contain the spiritual wisdom not of one individual, but of many people over great periods of time. They are not the religious revelation of one man which has been worked and reworked to become so far from the original as to have lost all truth. They are the living breathing dreams of the Gods, sent to show us the way to our true destiny, which is to rest once more in unity and harmony with the Divine forces of Heaven and Earth.

Pagan religion is all around us – in the landscape moulded by generations before into sacred hill and standing stone, into sacred burial ground and holy mountain, places where generations and generations have walked honouring the Gods of their peoples and their lands. It is a religion preserved in folk song and dance and in seasonal custom. We weave our corn dollies, we bob for apples at Hallowe'en, not remembering that these are the remnants of the religious celebrations of our ancestors the Celts, the Germani and the other myriad tribes who make up our Western inheritance.

As we enter the new millennium, we are seeing a rebirth of ancient spiritual traditions. The ancient Gods and Goddesses have slept for a while and are now awakening. Paganism is once again practised throughout Europe, North America, Australia and New Zealand. It is an official state religion in Iceland. The traditions that are practised are not only those of Europe. People all over the world are rejecting newer religions and returning to the wisdom of their ancestors.

Some Pagans worship the Gods of their ancestors or of the land in which they live. With the vast movements of populations we have seen throughout the past 200 or 300 years, these may no longer be the same. We may find we respond inwardly to a Deity that is not of our land or racial heritage. Many people all over the world are drawn to the Egyptian Deities. Some Pagans draw on a number of different religious traditions. They may worship the Great Mother Goddess, seeing all the different forms in which She has been worshipped all over the world as aspects of one Deity. Others may honour chiefly Odin or Cernunnos.

Some worshippers of the Pagan Gods describe themselves simply as Pagans, Heathens, Goddess worshippers or members of the Old Religion. Others follow particular traditions within Paganism. One of the most well known is Druidry or Druidism. The Druids were the priesthood of the Celts and great poets and healers. There are many groups which study the ancient skills of Druidry and worship its Gods. Others described themselves as Odinists, followers of Odin, or Asatru, followers of the High Gods of North Europe of whom Odin is chief. Others say they are followers of WiseCraft or Witchcraft . This is not the Witchcraft of Black Masses and Devil-worship, but the true WiseCraft of the land. It is a Medicine and Blessing Way, which honours the Gods and practises magic, healing crafts and the sight – those latent psychic abilities within us all which recent centuries have sought to suppress. Some call themselves Wiccan, a form of WiseCraft that honours the Great Mother Goddess and Horned God but also draws its inspiration from the Mystery Religions of the ancient world which taught our ancestors the way to self-knowledge and knowledge of the Gods. Other Pagans practise the Mysteries of the ancient Greeks or of Mithras, the Sun God of the Roman soldiery. In North America, many turn for inspiration to Native American spirituality, perhaps because they have Native American ancestry and feel a need to return to their ancient heritage, or because this spirituality is rooted in the land to which their ancestors emigrated. Although the forms in which the Gods are worshipped vary, there is sufficient commonality for them all to recognize themselves as part of the growing spiritual movement that is Paganism.

PAGANISM REBORN

How do people come to Paganism? Many of us grow up with a sense that Nature is sacred and Divine. It is natural for children to make altars in the woods and to honour the spirits of the trees, in the same way that children everywhere make sand castles upon the beach. We do not need to be taught these things, though some of us are. As we grow up, many of us forget the sense of sacred presence in tree or stream or by the sea, but some do not. Many of us find that we turn our prayers spontaneously to the Goddess or to the Great Spirit; that the Gods we find in our city temples and churches are not the Gods that speak to us in our dreams and visions. Often we feel lonely, believing no one else shares our sense of mystery and wonder.

With other children we learn the myths of our ancestors at school, but for us these stories are not ancient history. They are alive and meaningful. We learn that centuries before our ancestors honoured the Gods of sky and wind, of sun and rain; and that they honoured not only Gods but Goddesses. We learn that once Goddesses were honoured and respected. They ruled battle and war, wisdom and learning, as well as those things which in recent centuries have been thought of as belonging to the realm of women – the hearth and home, childbirth and motherhood.

Many of us may have felt that a change was in the air. In adulthood we may have called it 'a change of group consciousness'. The old Gods were waking. They filled our dreams and we wrote stories about them. Perhaps we painted their images. Perhaps we sensed that others felt this too. It may not have been our friends and relations, or perhaps it was. It may have been the authors of books shelved under fantasy and science fiction. Perhaps we read Marion Zimmer Bradley's book *The Mists of Avalon* (Sphere Books, 1984) with its honouring of the role of bard, priestess and Goddess. We knew that this was not history as it was, but perhaps history as it might have been. We dreamed of a world where the Goddess could be made manifest and the ancient Gods of hill and forest were honoured. If we are Native American, perhaps we read of the ancient ways of our grandfathers and grandmothers – of the Blessing Way, the Medicine Way. If we are Celts, we read the myths of our Celtic Deities. For others, the myths of the Norse *Eddas* (which means 'great-grandmother') seemed to speak with a power and resonance which the religion we were taught as children lacked.

There may be clues which led us to discover that we are not

strange or otherworldly or bound up in a forgotten past, but that we are Pagans. We may have read a book about modern Paganism, heard a radio interview, read a magazine article, or met someone through work or college who said, 'I am a Pagan,' and we knew then that we were too.

We are not alone. All over the world there are others worshipping the ancient Gods, honouring the powers of soul and spirit, the powers of magic and myth. Many of us may have felt a sense of recognition and of *déjà vu*, of coming home after a long journey – we have returned from a long exile to our own people. Many may have felt they were Pagans in a former life – perhaps Druid, Shaman, priestess or wise woman Witch. Perhaps this label describes what they feel they are today and what they seek to be. They may have a sense of vocation, of being called by the Gods. They may meet others of like mind by chance or by pursuing advertisements in Pagan journals or esoteric book stores. Perhaps they study with others who teach the Pagan mysteries. Perhaps they choose to pursue their path alone. Whatever their future path, they will share a common sense of arrival, of being now in their rightful place. They will have returned to the Ancient Ways that now speak to the future. They will have come home.

One of the reasons people who come into Paganism often have a sense of *déjà vu* is that we all inherit a collective human memory. Pagans believe that spiritual knowledge unfolds from within ourselves. To gain it, we must access that deeper layer of the mind that is the collective unconscious and contains the full repository of all human knowledge, past, present and that which has yet to be revealed. Much important knowledge has been lost to conscious memory. We have forgotten how to read the book of Nature. Our Western eyes look out on the Arizona desert and we see just that – desert. What we do not see is a storehouse of food, water and medicinal plants which could be used for every human ailment including cancer and for contraception. Modern human beings have scorned the 'primitives' who knew these things, but animals know more than we. Jungle elephants have inherited memory of 1,000 different plants which can be eaten for different illnesses. This is carried in the group memory of the species. How many humans are born with this type of knowledge?

Paganism teaches that knowledge is within us because we have a species memory. This was known to our ancestors but was largely forgotten until the psychologist Carl Jung discovered or remembered it and called it the collective unconscious. It was to this collective species memory that Shamans travelled to learn to cure illness. After a deep Shamanic experience, the individual was dismembered, reborn and returned from the Otherworld with intrinsic knowledge. *Dismembering* means tearing apart. *Remembering* is putting together again. This is what we must do to rediscover our ancient Pagan ways. In WiseCraft there is a saying: *If that which thou seekest thou findest not within thee, thou shalt never find it without thee.* This means that all esoteric knowledge is within us if only we can re-member it – re-assemble it from deep within our unconscious minds. Much of the school learning that we undertake is training the conscious mind to absorb external facts through reading and listening to others. This is useful, but we are taught this at the expense of a deeper knowledge, which is how to access to inherited core of knowledge and myth within us.

The hidden core of knowledge is accessed by lowering the barriers between the conscious and unconscious mind. This is what happens spontaneously in dreams and many scientific advances have been dreamt by their originators, who have then had to work backwards through the process of logical deduction to find out how they got there!

Scientific advances are also interesting because they give rise to great debates about ownership. Often a number of scientists working in different parts of the world will come to the same realization at the same time. This is because the group mind of humanity has advanced to such a point that this is the next logical step. However, it makes debates about ownership of ideas tricky. In the West we have been taught an individualistic stance which means that we 'own' ideas, a concept which would be foreign to our ancestors. Many of us who write, paint, compose and invent will have had the experience of beginning to dream a new idea or creation and being woken up in the night to receive what seems like astral dictation. The great bards and skalds of our ancestors did not believe that they owned the poems and sagas which came to them from dream and vision. They were seen as being sent by the Gods. The bards were only the human transmitters which received them and tried to record them as faithfully as possible.

Access to the timeless zone of the collective comes from learning the techniques of meditation and finding an interior stillness within ourselves where we can commune with the Gods and hear their voices penetrating the veil between the conscious and unconscious mind. It is achieving this connection with the deeper level of the Divine Self within us all which is the root of our Paganism.

DISPELLING MYTHS

The word 'Pagan' can arouse prejudice and fear and there is much misunderstanding of what Paganism represents. Let us examine some of the myths.

Paganism does not mean materialism.
A British Catholic bishop recently wrote in a Catholic newspaper that to open stores on Sundays was 'Pagan'. This is not Paganism but *secularism* and *consumerism*.

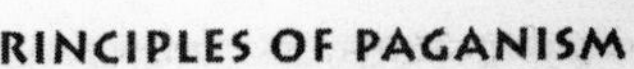

Pagans believe that it is good for all of us to have days that are focused on worship and leisure rather than on working and earning money. The only difference is that Pagans may not think that these days have to be Sundays. Pagans believe that the emphasis in modern society on consumerism may enrich us materially, but it leads to spiritual impoverishment and enriches us at the expense of the generations which follow. The resources of the Earth are not infinite. There is more to life than 'shopping 'til we drop'. Our material needs are important, but to pursue them without limit is counter-productive, for material things alone will not satisfy our deeper needs. The spirit too needs sustenance.

Pagans are not sexually degenerate.
They may, unlike Christians, believe that sex between consenting adults is natural and permissible provided both parties take sensible and mature safeguards against emotional exploitation, unwanted pregnancy and health hazards. They do not, however, believe in sex with goats or those under the legal age of consent. In fact, Pagan sexual morality is usually stricter than that practised in secular society.

Pagans are not anti-Christian.
They do not believe themselves that Christianity is the best religion for all, but they respect the fact that it is seen by many as a valid spiritual path. Where Paganism would not agree with Christianity, or with Islam, Buddhism or any other '-ism' is that these other paths are the *best* or *only* way for humans to honour and worship the Gods.

Some Pagans practise WiseCraft or Witchcraft, but Pagans are not Satanists.

Satan is the name given to the demon of Christianity and Paganism pre-existed Christianity by thousands of years. Those who are Witches in Paganism worship the ancient Gods and Goddesses of our lands and practise the healing and magical arts in order to help individuals, society and the environment around them.

Paganism does not advocate Black Magic or animal sacrifice.

Anyone seeking to use magic to gain power over others or for material ends would be better advised to apply elsewhere! Most Pagans believe that the human mind has powers that are as yet little understood. These are the power to transmit thought, the power to see the future, and the power to effect change by the use of love and will. These powers can only, however, be used in ways that are acceptable to the Gods; that is, in ways that benefit humankind and other forms of creation, not in ways which cause harm.

Now we have examined the myths, what do Pagans believe?

PAGAN BELIEFS

Pagans have a variety of beliefs, but at their core are three which many would share:

1) The Divine has made Itself manifest through many Deities in different places and at different times. No one Deity can express the totality of the Divine. This can be called *polytheism* – the Gods are many.

2) The Divine is present in Nature and in each one of us. This can be called *pantheism* – the Divine is everywhere.

3) *Goddess and God:* The Divine is represented as both female (Goddess) and male (God) while understanding that It is beyond the limitations of gender.

4) A fourth principle that some Pagans would share is called the *Pagan Ethic*: 'If it harms none, do what you will.'

POLYTHEISM

It has been easy in the past for the simple to believe that their version of religion was right, true, self-evidently good, the only acceptable truth and that people of other languages and races who held different beliefs were primitive, wrong-headed, misguided or simply evil. This way of thinking was as common in political as in religious life. It caused misery to millions. Over the centuries, it has been variously women, the Jews, new Christian sects, Pagans, Witches or People of Colour who were wrong, corrupt and had to be oppressed for their own good. The horrors of colonialism, Stalinism, Nazism, sexism, the Inquisition and racism wer[illegible]unched on one section of the population by another – not [illegible] main by those who sought deliberately to commit evil, bu[illegible]hose who were so deluded by their own doctrines and prop[illegible]da that they believed they were doing good. They were 'sav[illegible]r souls', 'protecting civilization', 'keeping the genetic sto[illegible]re' or doing it for the 'greater good of the Cause'. This is [illegible]*lusion of Rightness.*

Paganism does not teach that there[illegible]y one right way to worship the Divine or that the teaching[illegible]one particular racial group are superior to another. We do not seek to *export* our religions and foist them on others through force, bribery or fear. Polytheism means that we can respect the Gods of others and recognize in them another beauteous manifestation of the Divine force. Others worship their Gods in different ways from those which we use ourselves, but we do not start religious wars over the names of our Gods, or whether when we commune with them we eat of their bodies or of their bounty. Our Gods have a wider vision and seek us to grow towards them in individual understanding, not to impose on others ridiculous doctrines or to interpret literally what was meant to be understood as symbolic.

To Pagans, the Divine has manifested in different ways at different times to suit different peoples. With our limited human understanding, we have sought to encode and dogmatize these manifestations and to impose our interpretations on others. This is folly, for the Divine is beyond the limitations of our human minds and dogmas. Pagans believe that truth is revealed to each of us from deep within ourselves and must be sought through meditation and contemplation. It will express itself in forms and images that we can understand. These forms and images are like children's picture book versions of reality – an approximation but not a full exposition of the real thing.

Killing, maiming and torturing others in order to convince ourselves that one human-made image of the infinite reality is superior to that of another would be ridiculous if it were not so terrible and tragic.

The various Pagan polytheisms are therefore religions of tolerance. A Norse priestess who has become known in history as Sigrid the Proud explained to the Christian missionaries who sought to convert her:

I must not depart from the faith which I have held,
and my ancestors before me;
on the other hand, I shall make no objection
to your believing in the God that pleases you best.

Pagans worship the ancient Gods, but we are not harking back to a romantic past. We believe that in the past and in our ancient Gods lie keys to understanding the future. We also believe that human society is like a tree. It cannot live in midair. It must be rooted in the Earth and the Gods of the Earth and it must be rooted in an understanding of the past – both its wisdom and its mistakes.

Another besetting folly of humankind is the *Delusion of Stasis* – we think the world is static and unchanging. All scientific evidence is to the contrary – time and change march on, the seasonal cycle turns and turns again, we age. Yet always we wish to stop the passage of time. We cling to that which is outworn and has lost its usefulness; but to cling to stasis is to cling to illusion, for the message of the cosmos is change.

The law of change means that our religious forms and visions must evolve as society evolves and changes. New situations create new spiritual needs. The old temples must be rebuilt, the old forms of religion revived and revised. Symbols that have become mundane and meaningless must be refreshed by a return to the source of religious inspiration – contact with the Gods themselves. This means that we must all of us go deep into ourselves, into the storehouse of collective memory which is our human inheritance and meet there with our Gods and hear their voices. The Pagan traditions are not religions whose teachings are engraved on tablets of stone. Paganism is not promulgated by religious leaders who believe their thoughts and deeds are *infallible* – incapable of being wrong. Pagans take a humbler view. One American Druid order, Ar nDraiocht Fein (ADF), has proclaimed its first dogma – the *Doctrine of Archdruidic Fallibility*.

PANTHEISM

Paganism venerates the force of life itself, which is continually unfolding, renewing, disintegrating, returning to its source, resting and then awakening and renewing again. From its most simple beginnings, the universe has expanded outwards in ever-increasing complexity, seeking to know itself and to understand its own nature. Many Pagans believe in a conscious and creative universe in which humans and other creation are the eyes and ears, the brain and hands. All our experience is fed into the group mind of humanity which in turn feeds the consciousness of the universe. Some religions believe human beings are the only creation which is taking part in the this process. Pagans know that we are not. Each animal, plant and mineral life form has memory which it passes on to its own species and which it communicates to other species. Modern biologists support this view.

To Pagans, it is important to remember and honour the force which gives rise to us and sustains us. Life and consciousness are precious gifts and so too is the natural world of which we are a part. Often we forget and feel not *a part* but *apart*. We experience the *Delusion of Separateness*. We feel isolated and alone, our lives without meaning. The purpose of Paganism is to remind us of who and what we are; to celebrate the joy of life, so often masked with sorrow; and to honour the Gods, the great forces of the Universe, which give us life.

The Divine is like the breath of the universe that gives rise to the force of life itself. The Divine is within the air we breathe, the water we drink, the human, animal and plant life all around us. Just as we are spirits who inhabit a body, so too does the Divine inhabit the universe around us.

These pantheistic beliefs – that the Divine is in Nature – were natural to our ancestors. Today we live in a world of perpetual light, from the daylight outside to the electric light that we use to hold back the dark. Around our cities are great fiery glows that dim the wonders of the night sky and what we have not blotted out with electricity we have masked with our pollution. To our ancestors, however, the powers of the stars and planets above were an intimate part of their lives. They read the colour of the Moon and the movements of the stars to know what the weather would bring. They knew the certain Moon phases were better for planting, that certain winds would bring rain and the harvest must be gathered quickly, that the snows would bring the movement of herds to the hunter's bow. It was natural therefore for our ancestors to see the powers of the Gods made manifest in the ever-changing cloak of Nature. They realized that the tides and seasons were moved by a power greater than themselves and they honoured it by calling it 'Goddess' or 'God'.

Today, for many of us Nature is devoid of spirit. The monotheistic religions have desanctified it. They have moved the Divinity *upstairs*, to a spiritual and insubstantial realm. Our hearts no longer give thanks to the Goddess when the flowers bloom, when our crops thrive. We give thanks to weed killer and phosphates! Unfortunately, this so-called rational rather than reverential attitude to Nature is disastrous for our future. We are encouraged to exploit Nature and to overturn her balance, to cut down and burn precious resources which cannot be renewed for thousands of years. We alter our seasons, suspend our rainfall, turn the verdant plains into arid desert and believe that we are *making progress* even as we are sinking into the grossest stupidity. We move to the desert, but do not make desert gardens full of beautifully flowering cacti. We do not have the imagination. Instead we buy our gardens from a consumer's catalogue and lower the water table to create bright green grass, golf courses and palm trees where none ever grew before.

All this may suggest that Paganism is advocating a return to a romantic eco-friendly past, but Paganism is a practical religion concerned with the problems of the present. The change in world-view that has been advocated throughout the nineteenth and twentieth centuries by Paganism is now being adopted by those most pragmatic of organizations – insurance companies. In 1995 a high-level delegation from the international insurers Lloyd's of London visited an international climate conference in Berlin. Throughout the 1990s, insurers suffered dramatic and catastrophic losses as a result of natural calamities caused by global warming. Giant floods devastated the United States in 1993 and the Netherlands and China in 1995. Nine American insurance companies collapsed after Hurricanes Andrew and Iniki hit Florida and Hawaii in 1992. Twenty-four reinsurers pulled out of the Caribbean after the area was battered by storms. American Re, the third largest American reinsurer, has already set up a company to develop environmentally friendly technologies and is inviting solar power companies to offer themselves for investment. In Britain, the leaders of Britain's insurance corporations were told in a confidential report not to expect any help in their endeavours: the fossil-fuel industries are likely to 'effectively emasculate any measures that might be taken'. The insurance industry is having to go it alone.

The world is finally waking up to the disastrous and irresponsible attitude that the exploitation of our planet is causing and is now listening to the message which has long been put out by Paganism – to stop and think. We must take notice of our environment. We must honour the life forms which have lived there for millennia. We must not upset Nature's balance without understanding what we do. Paganism is a green religion. It encourages us to live in love and kinship with the natural world. The world was not created by the Gods for our benefit. We are but one of the billions of species through which the Gods have made manifest their creation. Our task is to take from the Earth what we need, leaving for other life forms that which we do not, and to honour the Gods who have provided for us a world of infinite beauty.

Some of the concerns of Paganism are those of what is known as deep ecology. Deep ecology is concerned with the connectedness between human beings and the rest of the planetary system. Connectedness is an important concept in Paganism and is the opposite of the Delusion of Separateness. We are part of Nature – cells in a functioning whole. Instead of perceiving the universe to be anthropocentric and available to be exploited to meet the needs of human beings, Paganism sees it as holistic and having its own purposes in which human beings play only a part.

What deep ecology often fails to address is the relationship between anthropocentric oppression of Nature and other forms of oppression. An important aspect of this has been the repression in spirituality, philosophy and society of the feminine.

The newer religions of the past two millennia are based on a fundamental error: that the Divine can be depicted as male and solely male. This is a strange and nonsensical belief if only we stop to think about it. The Divine has manifested over the ages as both Goddess and God to help us understand Its manifold complexity. If we worship only one half of the Divine, then understanding will be lost. We disenfranchise half of our fellows. We say that God is made in our image and not in yours; our sex is Divinely ordained to control, exploit and abuse yours; or else to enthrone you, remove you from interaction in the world of the everyday; to confine you to the home, to heaven, to the world of the womb; to deny you intellectual outlet or spiritual satisfaction.

Paganism teaches that both women and men, girls and boys, Goddess and God are equally valuable and necessary to a balanced and whole society and creation. Paganism teaches that to be a whole man is to be strong, powerful, loving, generous, gentle and nurturing. It does not imprison us in a strait-jacket of sexually stereotyped behaviour that denies on the one hand to women their power to interact in the world and on the other to men the power to express love and caring.

Feminism in the nineteenth and twentieth centuries gave a strong impetus to the worship of the Goddess. Both men and women were inspired to question and reject the limitation of patriarchal monotheisms.

A great deal of the misogyny present in monotheistic religion has been due to its negative attitude towards the body. In

Paganism the body is considered the temple of the Divine spark within us. Our senses relay to us the beauties of the physical world, which is a manifestation of the Divine force. Nature is therefore good and so too is the physical realm. Union with the Divine is to be sought in the material world, not only in the spiritual realm beyond. The body need not be a distraction from spirituality.

The past millennium in the West has been dominated by a Christian ethos which has had very negative attitudes to sex. Religion taught that celibacy was better than marriage and that sexual activity, particularly women's sexual activity, had to be tightly controlled. If sex is sinful, then that which arouses sexual desire is sinful. For man, it is woman who most arouses his sexuality – therefore woman is evil and sinful. Man can best be protected from woman by segregating her and subjugating her. This is, of course, a simplistic analysis. There are many other complex historical and economic causes for women's suppression, but recent religious symbolism has encouraged rather than counteracted them.

PAGAN ETHICS

Paganism does not have a complex set of commandments, but teaches that we must examine our conduct in the light of a simple meta-rule: if it harms none, it is permissible. We must ask ourselves, 'What impact will my actions have on others? Will they cause hurt or harm? Can I do this, take this, say this without damage to other human beings, other species, the planet itself?' This is the way of *least harm*.

Pagans recognize that the very existence of the human race is a threat to the rest of the planet's creation. We are greedy for resources, we exploit other species and give little in return. Yet exist we do and our continued existence lies in ensuring that we steer our society towards those values that are likely to preserve not only the human race but also the planet around us.

Giving something back to the Earth in return for the life she gives us is important in Paganism and is found throughout Pagan thought. One old Pagan prayer from Lithuania (one of the last countries in Europe to be Christianized) speaks of planting trees of thanks. When a child is born, when there is a marriage or any other joyous event, we can celebrate by planting trees.

Not all of us own land or gardens in which to plant trees, but a way in which we can practise our Paganism is to join organizations that do. There are now bodies in many countries which are dedicated to tree planting and to buying forests and woodlands in order to conserve them. These are all ways by which we can replenish Nature. We may feel that our contribution is very small, but we can not only do something ourselves, we can encourage others to do the same. Performing even a small right action is like throwing a stone into a pond. It plants ideas in the minds of others and they too can pass those ideas on.

Grass roots community action is very much a part of how society is operating today in many developed countries. People can no longer rely on large-scale bodies such as governments to do what is needful. People are banding together to say that we must do something ourselves. This is not the prerogative of Paganism but is a way forward for many. Maybe we cannot afford to buy land or woodland ourselves, but if we talk about these ideas to friends, relatives, fellow Pagans, we may find others like us who see these things as important and can contribute small amounts. Over time, these amounts will grow until we can perhaps preserve a woodland by purchasing it and provide not only trees with a permanent home but also have a site which can be used for ritual space, camping to attune to the land and other ways in which we can express our Paganism.

At one time, trees were planted to ensure a ready supply of firewood and timber for building and furniture. These are still important needs, but in this time of major deforestation, trees are essential to maintain the very air that we breathe. The great forests of the world are part of the Earth's ecosystem and create oxygen in the atmosphere. They are also essential for maintaining rainfall all over the globe. So when we destroy trees in one part of the world in another we inflict drought. Our failure to understand this stems from our Delusion of Separateness. It is hard for the human mind to conceive that what we think and do can have such far-reaching effects, but people are beginning to understand this through Chaos Theory, a scientific theory which argues that a small change in one part of the globe, say, the fluttering of a butterfly's wing, will have millions of knock-on effects which can result in a hurricane in another part of the world. This type of advanced scientific thinking is beyond the grasp of most of us, but if we accept it and start to think about and question our own behaviour in this light, then we will come to realize that everything we say and do impinges on the other human beings and life forms around us. We cannot cease to create what Buddhists call *karma* – all our actions have effects and implications that we cannot foresee – but we can do our best to ensure that we try to live lives that do least harm to those around us. This is a somewhat less ambitious ethos than attempting to do good, but it is an important one.

Conserving Nature means preserving the beautiful diversity with which our Gods have seen fit to furnish us. We do not yet understand the complex interaction of our biosphere and the role which each life form has to play in its maintenance. All we know is our own ignorance. We meddle with this balance at our peril because we do not understand and for this reason it is important that we preserve the diversity of species as much as we can. Active Pagans are involved not only in land conserva-

so in animal conservation and animal rights. The at to inflict cruelty and pain on other species just becau they are less powerful than we are is wrong. It is not only wrong from the point of view of the animals concerned – it is also very bad for humans because it sends to us and our heirs the wrong messages. When we practise cruelty to animals, we will also practise cruelty to other human beings, especially those who are more vulnerable than we. In learning responsibility to other species we also learn to respect boundaries and individuality of others. This is important if we are to survive as a species. Many Pagans are vegetarians and many others restrict themselves to free-range meat, but this is not because they are practising asceticism and see it as benefiting their spiritual well-being (though it may). They prefer to forgo meat because they believe large-scale factory farming and meat production are harmful to the planet and cruel to other species.

We harm the planet because we do not understand our intimate connection with it, but our separation is not only from the world of Nature, it is also from one another. Pagans believe that the way society today teaches us to relate to one another is in many ways wrong. We are taught a rampant, 'me first' individualism. We are taught to consume as much as possible without thought of the consequences for others, both now and in the future. This is because we have lost the ties of kinship and clan which once bound us to other people. Often today other people seem strange, threatening, 'other', different and apart. This is most true of those of other races, other beliefs and other tongues, but it is also true of our neighbours and of those around us. We live in a world which is the most densely populated it has ever been, but many of whose people are alienated, isolated and lonely. Paganism teaches that we are not separate and alone. We are each plants from a common root, though this is hidden below the surface of our conscious minds, in the

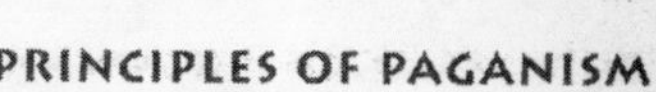

collective unconscious. So if we hurt another person, ultimately we hurt ourselves; for at a layer of our psyche deeper than any of us can understand, we are no longer separate. We are one.

Our connectedness means that mutual help and aid are important in Paganism. Paganism teaches that society supports and nurtures us. In return, we must support and nurture others. Marxism, while an atheist philosophy, had a rule that was more honoured in the breach than the observance, but its original ethos was one with which all spiritual traditions would accord: *From each according to his or her means and to each according to his or her needs*. In other words, we must all give to society according to our talents and strengths and in return we will receive that which meets our needs.

In the *Eddas*, the religious writings of our Northern European ancestors, we are told that each human being is valuable and can offer something to society; whether we are able-bodied or weak, whatever disability may afflict us, there is still something which we can contribute:

A lame man can ride; a handless herd cattle,
a deaf man may be a fine warrior.
Better be blind than burn on the pyre;
no one needs a corpse.

THE *Hávamál* OR HIGH ONE'S WORDS, V.71.

This is a philosophy of optimism and hope that can comfort us when we feel least worthy, least able to have anything to offer, most in despair.

BALANCE AND HARMONY

'Balance' and 'harmony' are key words to an understanding of Paganism. No quality in excess is good. We must learn to use each quality skilfully – in its own due place. Inevitably at times, we will fail. Sometimes we will fail badly. No one has all the answers and in trying to answer the questions and meet the challenges of life we will often get it wrong. All of us will succumb at various points in our lives to the all too common human failings and delusions. We will give way to our less worthy impulses and perform actions which hurt and harm others. Sometimes this will be deliberate. Other times it will be due to ignorance or lack of thought. What happens when we fail? Guilt, worry and breast-beating will not help. In the Norse *Eddas* the God Odin gives this advice:

A fool lies awake at nights, worrying of this and that;
weary is he when morning breaks, and all remains as before.

THE *Hávamál* OR HIGH ONE'S WORDS, V.23.

First we must accept that we are less than perfect, much less than perfect. This is challenging, for it requires us to live with an image of ourselves that may be very different from what we would wish. Above the doors of an ancient Greek mystery temple were the words 'Know Thyself.' This means knowing that deep within us is a Divine spark, part of the greater Divine whole to which ultimately we will return. Surrounding this Divine spark are layers of dross that we would much rather pretend have nothing to do with us at all.

Knowing ourselves means being realistic about ourselves and about others. All of us will get things wrong. Having done so, we must forgive ourselves and start again. To start again, we must seek to redress the balance and to give something back in return for what we have taken or abused. This may not be directly. What we have done may not always be undone. However, we can seek to redress the balance by contributing positive energy and action where we have contributed negative.

This may not be in the same time or place, or for the same people but, in the great weighing of the balance, equilibrium can again be found.

One way of helping us live a balanced and harmonious life is to practise honour and truth. These are important concepts in Paganism. The *Eddas* teach that:

Cattle die, kinsmen die; you yourself will die;
but honour never dies, for one who has earned a good name.

THE *Hávamál* OR HIGH ONE'S WORDS, V.76.

Strong societies are built on trust, honour and honesty. To lie, cheat and steal create mistrust and deceit that destroy the fabric of society. Our Celtic ancestors believed that Nature herself was witness to our truthfulness and would act against us if we broke with the way of harmony and balance that truthfulness implies. The Celts who fought with the Macedonian conqueror Alexander the Great swore to him on the eve of battle:

If we observe not this engagement,
may the sky fall on us and crush us,
may the Earth gape and swallow us up,
may the sea burst out and overwhelm us.

A thousand years later in Ireland, in the epic poem *Tain bo Cualigne,* The Brown Bull of Quelgny, almost the same oath is sworn by the Ulstermen to their king:

Heaven is above us
and the Earth beneath us,
and the sea around us.
Unless the sky shall fall with its showers of stars
on the ground where we are camped,

or unless the Earth shall be rent by earthquake,
or unless the waves of the blue sea
come over the forests of the living world,
we shall not give ground.

By keeping our word, our honour and our truth, the world of Nature will bless and preserve us. We also help to evolve humanity as a whole. Each human being is like a wave in the great ocean which is the collective mind of the human race. Negative thoughts, words and deeds are like pollutants in the great ocean of being. They hurt others and they also hurt and contaminate us. The metaphor of the ocean also helps us understand that separate we are weak but acting together in communities we are strong. One wave alone is lost upon the shore and dissolves into the sand, leaving not a trace; but the power of the ocean will wear away the hardest granite cliff.

To live a balanced life we must also consider the way in which we live. 'Right livelihood' is a Buddhist phrase, but one that is equally applicable to Pagans.

The aims of some multi-national corporations and their environmental impact do not match the ethos of Paganism. This does not mean that Pagans do not operate in the business world. In fact, the more the better, but Paganism does not place the profit motive above all else. Longer term considerations such as building equitable and just societies and the continuation of our planet and as many as possible of the species within it – there is beauty and strength in diversity – are more important.

Apart from this, one Pagan's definition of right livelihood may not be the same as another's. There are many Pagans in the military. Conversely, peace and anti-nuclear campaigning were two of the major routes into Paganism in the 1970s and 1980s. Around half the Pagan community is vegetarian. Other

Pagans rear and slaughter their own animals. These are all very emotive issues which test tolerance between Pagans. These tensions teach us to examine and question our motives and the morality of what we do, often in the light of the meta-principle of: what will contribute to the greater good? Each influx of new groups into Paganism raises new moral issues and helps us all to question, define and redefine what it means to be a Pagan today.

There are actions that we consider good and rightful and actions that are harmful and damaging. Many religions call these good vs evil or sin, but these terms are used less by Pagans. The emphasis in Paganism is not on sin but on ethics, on learning a body of basic principles by which to make judgements about our thoughts and deeds. Evil in Paganism is generally seen not as arising from the cosmic forces of the universe, but from the actions of human beings. The delusions that beset humanity and prevent us from seeing the Divine reality around us cloud our judgement. It is our task to achieve the original meaning of *clairvoyance* – clear seeing. We approach clear-seeing by asking ourselves each day if our thoughts, actions, words, feelings are in accord with the Pagan Ethic of 'If it harms none, do what you will.'

Most Pagans would also go beyond this to its converse: evil must not be allowed to go unchecked. Tolerance is an important aspect of Paganism, but it does not mean tolerance of evil. Oppression and suppression of one part of the population by another and religious and political regimes that support this are wrong. It is important to remember that democracy was a Pagan invention devised by the ancient Greeks. Authoritarian religions tend to support authoritarian political regimes that practise racism, sexism and oppression of anyone who dissents. These manifestations become particularly apparent when religion is in control of the state. The principles of

Paganism are in accord with a secular state in which all have a democratic voice and which allows religious freedom to all, while ensuring that those religions do not deny the basic rights of human self-determination to their members. In order to have such a state, channels of communication and peaceful protest must be in place. Systems that allow the media to be dominated by particular religious, political and corporate interests and which prevent ordinary people from expressing dissent to government policy do not accord with 'if it harms none' because they take no account of the legitimate concerns of the people.

LIFE AND DEATH

The ethics of Paganism are part of a Pagan view of life and death. Paganism differs from many religions in its attitude to the created world. Since Nature is a manifestation of the Divine and life on Earth is a pleasure and a gift, then we can be in union with the Divine in this life as well as in the one beyond.

This is not always easy. We often have difficulty reconciling ourselves to the fact that life is unfair. However fortunate our own circumstances, there are always others who are more successful and have better houses and cars, more interesting and better paid jobs, better behaved and more loving children and are better looking and more sexually successful than we are. The human mind has a gift for making itself miserable by looking constantly at what it does not have, rather than enjoying what it has. The Pagan ethos focuses on enjoying and celebrating the fact of life itself and the gift of consciousness which is a major miracle of the cosmos. There is no need to flee our Earth in order to enter into non-material bliss. We should celebrate and be thankful for our Earthly incarnation.

Life is balanced by death. What do Pagans believe about death? Most Pagan traditions teach reincarnation: our life on Earth is one of many and the purpose of life is to learn and

evolve. Reincarnation is often thought of as purely an Eastern teaching, but this is not the case. The Druids taught the transmigration of souls – that after death the soul would incarnate again. Some in the Norse–German tradition believe that we are born once only. Others believe that individuals bound together by ties of blood and love would be reborn to meet one another again. Traces of both beliefs are found in Northern European literature. What we decide about the nature of incarnation is for us alone, but it is important to remember that prior to Christianity the doctrine of reincarnation was a widely accepted belief about the after-life. Traces of this are found in the myths of all European peoples and also in some forms of early Christianity. There may have been many more which were suppressed by later unsympathetic recorders.

Irish mythology tells the beautiful story of Etain, who reincarnates as the wife of Eochy, High King of Ireland. Her previous husband, who dwells in the Otherworld, comes back to find her and appeals to her to return with him to the Otherworld – *Tir na N'Og*, the Land of Youth, which was also called The Great Plain. To the Celts, *Tir na N'Og* held no fears.

O fair-haired woman,
will you come with me
to the marvellous land, full of music,
where hair is primrose yellow
and skin whiter than snow?
There none speaks of 'mine' or 'thine' –
white are teeth and black are brows;
eyes flash with many-coloured lights,
and the hue of the foxglove is on every cheek.

Pleasant to the eyes are the plains of Erin,
but they are as a desert to the Great Plain.

Heady is the ale of Erin,
but the ale of the Great Plain is headier.
It is one of the wonders of that land
that youth does not change into age.
Smooth and sweet are the streams that flow through it;
mead and wine abound of every kind.
There men are all fair, without blemish;
there women conceive without sin.
We see around us on every side,
yet no one seeth us.
The cloud of Adam's sin hides us from their observation.

O Lady, if thou wilt come to my strong people,
the purest of gold shall be on thy head –
thy meat shall be pork unsalted,
new milk and mead shalt thou drink with me there,
O fair-haired woman.

Not all Pagans believe that they as individuals will live again. Many believe that their life essence is undying and will reform into new life, but this is more in the nature of material which is broken down and reused. They do not expect to remember previous incarnations but see each life experience as unique.

Some Pagans who believe in personal reincarnation have ideas similar to Hindus about karma: our lives are affected by the implications of our past actions. On a logical level this is obviously true – the old saying about chickens coming home to roost reflects this idea. Pagans who believe in reincarnation may also believe that we are born with a legacy of accumulated karma from past lives. These are the consequences of our actions before we are born. Other Pagans believe that although the life force and that spark within us which is part of it endure, transform and live again, the slate is washed clean and we do not carry the past forward with us.

The truth of this must be for the individual to decide from experience and logic. It is not a matter on which others should make pronouncements. Many of the ideas of retribution for sin and accumulated karma are ways to help us behave more properly in the present. They are the 'sticks' which are designed to help us mend our ways. Paganism tends to emphasize the 'carrot' rather than the stick – that we should behave in ways that are ethical and benefit society around us because this will make us happier and more fulfilled people in the present.

These are some Pagan beliefs, but who are today's Pagans?

THE PAGAN COMMUNITY

One of the most obvious things which strikes anyone who goes to a Pagan gathering is the diversity of the Pagan community. Walking around Avebury stone circle once with a Pagan group from London, I was surprised to notice that everyone was looking at us. Turning round to look at our party wending its way around the stones, I could see why. It was not that any one individual looked unusual, but it was the combination of elderly English ladies with walking sticks, middle-aged men in sports jackets, leather-jacketed Goths with pierced noses and Doc Marten boots, families carrying babies, hippies whose dress style had not changed since 1972, men with pony tails, men and women with hennaed hair, perms and shaven heads... Yes, collectively, we were an unusual group.

It is often a great relief to middle-aged and older Pagans to find that Paganism is not solely a young movement. In Europe at least there is a core of older people who have been practising Pagans since before the Second World War, but the Pagan movement began to grow enormously from the 1970s onwards. This might mean that it is primarily a young movement, but this is not the case. People tend to look at spirituality during periods in their lives when they have most time to think about themselves and where they are going. This may be when they are bringing up young children and have to teach them ethics and a spiritual framework in which to set them. This can be the time when they realize that their own spiritual life is deficient and that they need to do something about it. Often, however, people examine their spirituality either when they are young or else from middle age onwards, when they have more free time to indulge in such luxuries. Many people become Pagans in their twenties; many become Pagans in their forties, fifties or later.

Most Pagans will meet with other Pagans on some occasions during the year in order to mix with those of like mind and to exchange ideas, but this need not necessarily involve religious ceremony. Often gatherings will discuss ideas and people will return home to their own temples, groves and shrines to honour the Gods. Whereas in most religious groupings, the main contact between members will be at gatherings for worship, Pagans meet together often for summer camps, winter conferences and, in Britain especially, in pubs over pints of real ale in discussion gatherings known as pub moots. Gaining one's religious inspiration in a pub may seem odd to those used to more austere religious approaches, but Pagan religion is not pious in the way in which religion has been strait-jacketed in recent millennia.

Until recently, most people found their own way into Paganism rather than being brought up in Pagan families. This meant that Pagan celebrations were geared towards adults rather than children. This is now changing as people are raising their children as Pagans.

Introducing younger children to Paganism is relatively easy. Many children are natural Pagans and like rhythms, cycles, celebration and special customs, foods and games for special days. Paganism can be introduced in a non-pious way by keeping a household shrine and allowing children to decorate it appropriately throughout the season. Burning incense once a day or lighting candles as offerings to the Gods are very simple expressions of our relationship with the Divine which are nevertheless very evocative for Pagans of all ages. Useful books are now beginning to appear (although more are needed), which can help those raising Pagan children. Some of these are listed in Chapter 7.

COMMUNITY GROUPS

Paganism teaches that we are each responsible for ourselves. This means we must take responsibility for our own spiritual development. Others who travel the same path may offer us wisdom and advice, and particular Pagan traditions can sustain and help us, but in the end we must become our own teachers and guides.

Paganism does not have a central controlling body, Popes, bishops, imams who issue religious death sentences or any of the other paraphernalia of religious totalitarianism. There are, however, a number of Pagan organizations, staffed primarily by volunteers, which serve as information giving and networking bodies. These organizations may also produce magazines and run Pagan events such as annual gatherings, conferences,

seasonal celebrations or teaching workshops.

The main bodies in Europe are the Pagan Federation, run by a democratically elected committee, and the Fellowship of Isis. In Australia and New Zealand the main body is the Pan-Pacific Pagan Alliance. There is as yet no single representative body in North America but there are bodies that cover particular parts of the continent. There are also large organizations representing groups following particular Pagans paths such as Druidry, Wicca, Odinism/Asatru or the Paganism of particular ethnic communities. Some of these are listed at the end of this book *(see Chapter 7)*.

In North America, some organizations have, for tax and other legal reasons, created churches. These include the Aquarian Tabernacle Church and the Wiccan Church of Canada. Although they may use the name 'church', this does not mean that they seek converts. Pagans believe that those who are meant to be Pagan will find their own way to the ancient altars of the Gods, providing signposts are left by those who have walked the way before. Pagans rely on the books, magazines and information put out by their community to speak to those whose hearts are open, rather than seeking to convert people on street corners. Nor are the Pagan organizations cults whose members follow a particular religious leader, usually male, who has the only sure-fire way of getting on the last spaceship before the Apocalypse, the elixir of eternal youth, the key to limitless riches or the only 'true' Divine revelation (which can, of course, be transmitted through sex with its messenger). Such gurus usually choose to masquerade under a Christian or New Age front. Pagans tend to be individualists who are not prepared to follow such teachings.

No one needs to join a Pagan organization to become a Pagan, though many do. Often we want to meet with others to celebrate and worship together and to learn and share ideas.

However, we need no ceremony and we need not be 'saved', for there is nothing to be saved from. We need only to commit ourselves earnestly in our hearts to the ancient Deities of our lands and peoples and to announce to them alone that we are theirs. Some Pagan traditions and groups are very structured and are entered through a dedication, induction, initiation or adoption ceremony, but these rites are gateways into their own traditions and groups only. We can be Pagans without any of these ceremonies.

Pagans may worship alone much of the time, either from necessity or choice. Some Pagans prefer to practise a solitary Paganism. Some meet with other Pagans for rites of passage and seasonal celebrations on an ad hoc basis. Some belong to groups which meet together to honour the Gods on a regular basis. These groups may also engage in social, environmental and teaching activities. Some groups are geared to family Paganism; others cater for Pagans who prefer to worship in single sex groups and some groups are for adults who are practising an initiatory path. Pagans may belong to more than one of these.

In Britain and in many other countries, an evolutionary change took place during the 1980s and 1990s. Prior to this most Pagans came into Paganism via a specific Pagan tradition – usually Wicca, Druidry or the Northern Tradition. They identified first with their own tradition and only secondly with the Pagan community as a whole. This has now changed. In Europe, 50 per cent of the Pagan Federation's members consider their primary allegiance to be Paganism in general rather than a specific Pagan path. This has meant the growth of a healthy and eclectic Pagan tradition which has been assisted in its development by members of the specific Pagan paths who recognize that their path is not suitable for all those wishing to practise Paganism. The number of 'non-aligned' Pagans has

encouraged the growth of broad-based Pagan organizations and of open seasonal festivals where those of the specific traditions and those who classify themselves simply as 'Pagan' can meet together to worship the Gods.

Due to problems of size and geography, the United States has had greater difficulty in creating nation-wide Pagan umbrella organizations and as yet none have emerged. A more eclectic approach generally has also meant that Wicca and Druidry in the States have been able to accommodate a broader spectrum of Pagans than the equivalent organizations in Europe. The need for broad-based Pagan organizations has therefore been slower to develop.

How much difference is there between the various Pagan traditions?

Druidry and the Northern Tradition worship different pantheons, with Druidry being oriented towards Celtic Deities and the Northern Tradition towards those of German and Scandinavian Europe. Between the two traditions there are, however, similarities in that both believe their Deities are manifest in Nature, both have Goddesses and Gods, both have a role for the practice of divination and magic, both have a strong ecological ethos and both tend to favour structured groupings.

The ethos of different Pagan traditions can be deduced from the terminology used to describe its groups. In Druidry, the small groups are often known as 'groves', a word which conveys the importance in which Nature and sacred trees are held in the Druid Tradition. In the Northern Tradition, a group is often called a 'hearth'. The hearth was the centre of the home in ancient Northern Europe and the word conveys the importance in the Northern Tradition of family and kin. Wicca and WiseCraft groups are called 'covens', a word which derives from 'convene', which also gave rise to 'convent'. A convent is a place set apart and dedicated solely to union with the Divine.

The Druid groves are generally members of one of the Druid orders and Northern Tradition hearths of one of the Asatru or Odinist organizations. Wicca or WiseCraft is somewhat different in that it generally functions in small autonomous groups rather than larger organizations, although in the United States there are umbrella organizations. Wicca has some similarities with Druidry in that there is a Celtic orientation to its Deities, although these are not solely Celtic. In fact, since the emphasis in Wicca and the Craft is on worshipping the Goddesses and Gods of the land, it is possible to call upon Celtic or Northern European Deities according to one's location and personal preference.

DRESS

In everyday life, Pagans do not usually wear special forms of dress, but may wear distinctive jewellery in the same way that Jews will wear a Star of David or Christians a cross. Many Pagans wear pendants or rings of Celtic, Norse, Egyptian or esoteric origin which remind them of their Pagan affiliation. Those following the Northern Tradition (Odinism or Asatru) may wear the symbol of the Hammer of Thor. The three-legged symbol of the triskell is common amongst those who honour the Celtic Gods, the pentacle (five-pointed star) amongst followers of WiseCraft and the ankh amongst those honouring the Egyptian Gods and also amongst those following Wicca.

Hammer of Thor (Northern Tradition). Pentacle (Wicca/WiseCraft).

Ankh (Egyptian Tradition and Wicca). Triskell (Celtic Traditions).

A clue as to the focus of different Pagan traditions is found in their ritual dress. For religious rites, some Pagans wear their everyday clothes; others wear a special robe. Some branches of WiseCraft perform some of their rites 'skyclad' or naked in order to express their return to the world of innocence. The extent to which special dress is used reflects the orientation of the Pagan tradition involved – whether it is oriented outwards to family and social life or inwards to personal spiritual development. Those Pagan paths which by their dress (or undress) emphasize separateness are oriented more towards adult initiation into the Mysteries. Those whose rites may also take place in everyday clothes are more family oriented. Thus Druidry and Asatru carry out rites in either robes or everyday dress, whereas most branches of WiseCraft wear robes or nothing at all.

The reason for adopting a special form of dress for religious rites is to emphasize that we are entering a realm which is separate, though not wholly separate, from the everyday world. Wicca often speaks of its rites as taking place 'between the worlds' or 'between the realms of men and the realms of the Mighty Ones'. The Mighty Ones are revered ancestors who have gone before. A similar term, Mighty Powers, is used in the same sense in the texts of the *Eddas*.

In Paganism the word 'priest' or 'priestess' refers to someone who enacts a ritual function. In most traditions the aim is for all adults to learn to be priests or priestesses of their communities, unless of course that is not their wish. A Pagan priest or priestess will play a role in organizing seasonal rites and rites of passage and in teaching others who are new to Paganism about Pagan tradition and modern Paganism. However, he or she may or may not undertake some of the social functions which are associated with priesthoods in other religions.

Pagan communities vary in how organized they are and the extent to which they wish to take on functions of social work and spiritual ministry. This type of activity is, however, growing and the Pagan ethos is to provide help if asked. From this has arisen an external ministry, particularly in Britain, the United States and Canada. Many people turn to religion to comfort them, to help them find sense and meaning in their lives, and to help them plan for the future. People who are in prison have time to reflect upon the errors and processes which got them there and may decide to evolve a better philosophy and way of life. In some cases prisoners have turned to Paganism and prison authorities have turned to the Pagan community to help these newcomers to Paganism. In other cases, Pagans have become involved in hospital or student ministry because Pagans in hospitals and colleges have requested the aid of a more experienced Pagan in times of crisis, to provide counselling or guidance as to how to follow a Pagan path, or to help organize seasonal and other celebrations.

ORGANIZED AND DISORGANIZED PAGANISM

Often Paganism is deliberately spontaneous and unstructured. It arises out of individual spiritual experience. Although people might label themselves as Pagan, they might not wish to join any form of group or organization. Their honouring of the Gods is liable to take place either alone, on an ad hoc basis with friends or through large festivals and gatherings.

Some Pagans have reacted strongly against the patriarchal hierarchies of 'organized' religion and have sought not to make the same mistakes themselves. The solution has been either not to join groups or to create small leaderless groups which deliberately set out to foster 'power-from-within' rather than 'power-over'.

TECHNO-PAGANISM

From ecology to the Internet may seem a long leap, but Paganism is in every sense a very modern religion. It may be thought of as a revival of the ways of our ancestors, but we do not only find Pagans worshipping the Gods in woodland clearings. Some of the places people are most likely to meet other Pagans are at music festivals and on the Internet.

Computerized Paganism may seem at odd concept, but the Pagan community is one of the most computer-literate of religious groupings. Information technology specialists are the largest occupational grouping in Paganism. Quite why it should have such an appeal to those with information technology skills is a complex question, but one reason is that both worlds tend to attract intelligent individualists who question given assumptions. There are now Pagan bulletin boards where Pagans all over the world exchange views and information. Some of these are listed in Chapter 7.

SHAMANISM AND ANARCHO-PAGANISM

A number of Pagans would describe themselves as 'Shamans'. Shamans in tribal society were those who dealt with the Otherworld and other states of consciousness. In older societies, disease and community and individual problems were considered the result not only of causes on the material plane, but also of supernatural causes such as spirits. The job of the Shaman was to undertake the risky business of travelling into the Otherworld to discover the cause of an illness or other problem and to put it right. This might involve hunting down a spirit animal which was oppressing the victim or ridding the victim of an ancestral spirit which had possessed him or her.

To enter into the Otherworld, Shamans used special techniques of consciousness change. These involved drumming at specific beats which induce trance and out-of-body experience, fasting and hallucinogenic drugs derived from mushrooms and plants. Many people today who have experimented with hallucinogenic and soft drugs have discovered that these can produce altered perception and altered states of consciousness which include heightened awareness, synaesthesia – whereby we see sound and hear colour – and visions. Often these visions are very similar in content to those experienced by tribal Shamans and also by mystics. They often have a profound spiritual impact on those who experience them, but they may not know how to interpret their experience, what it means in terms of their spiritual life or how to achieve the same experiences without drug intervention. In tribal societies these took place in a spiritual context, which enable people to interpret them constructively and meaningfully and to use these insights to enhance their spiritual lives.

Many of those who have had such experiences today turn to Paganism with its understanding of Shamanic experience and its respect for the value of the insights gained from altered states of consciousness. This has brought an influx of younger people into Paganism, whose ideas have tended to be more radical and anarchistic than some of their older brothers and sisters. Staid Pagan conferences have found themselves ending not in silent meditation but Shamanic discos.

Rock and folk festivals will have a large Pagan contingent and Pagan bands have formed to incorporate ancient Pagan themes into modern music. At festivals, such as the Glastonbury Festival, performance art has met Pagan ritual to produce participative ritual focusing on simple but highly evocative themes through the use of fire mazes, wicker men, masks and dance. The images are of a modern tribal Paganism, a tribe not united by blood but by spirit. These Pagans most often do not join Pagan organizations. Their worship of the Gods is outdoor, ecstatic and spontaneous – created of the moment from the energy of the people present. It is as likely to take place at a rave or an environmental protest action as at a gathering formally designated as Pagan. It is a living and evolving Paganism which speaks of the future rather than the past, but is nevertheless rooted in our most basic religious urges – to dance, chant and drum for our Gods. The hippies of the 1970s went East for enlightenment. The anarcho-Pagans of the 1980s and 1990s couldn't afford it and stayed at home to find enlightenment had been on the doorstep all along.

ECO-PAGANISM

Those who have come to Paganism via Shamanistic and anarchist routes do not subscribe to materialistic and consumerist values. Their concerns are not consumption but conservation. Most Pagan traditions and groups are actively concerned with environmental issues through direct environmental campaigning and/or through the use of prayer and magic to change the attitude of society. In this, Western Pagans are not alone. All over the world, indigenous traditions and tribal peoples are working towards the same ends.

To meet such concerns, there are also Pagan groups which focus specifically on environmental issues. In Britain, the most active of these in the Dragon group, which supports practical action with Pagan magic to protect specific sites which are under threat from road-building programmes or other damage.

Environmental action is also a route by which many Pagans come to Paganism.

GODDESS GROUPS

Paganism's ecological stance is encouraged by its veneration for the Divine feminine – the Goddess – who has always been strongly associated with the world of Nature. The importance of the Goddess and women is a distinguishing feature of Paganism.

Some Pagan groups are dedicated particularly to the worship of the Goddess. The Fellowship of Isis, which is open to both men and women, is one of the largest of these and ordains both sexes as priests and priestesses of the Goddess. The Dianic branch of WiseCraft, named in honour of the Goddess Diana, is active particularly in the United States. Dianic Craft is matriarchal – women led. Some groups exclude men and see their tradition as a sisterhood, as 'wimmin's religion'. Other groups work with men, but see their role as less important than that of the women.

There are also informal groups of women who meet together to worship the Goddess. Some are modelled on Wicca. Other groups are Shamanic. Some blend aspects of classical Paganism, Native American spirituality and other traditions to create an eclectic worship of the Great Goddess geared to meet modern needs.

In the 1980s, many women became involved in Paganism through peace camps and peace campaigning, whereby they came to recognize that many of the negative attitudes which fostered weaponry and war were a direct result of an imbalance in society towards 'masculine' values of competitiveness and away from 'feminine' values of conservation and nurturing.

This led many women to question the religions of their childhood and in questioning them to find them wanting. Some women remained in their family's religious tradition but began actively campaigning for a greater recognition of the Divine feminine and for women's participation in the ministry. Other women decided that their religious ideas had evolved beyond the monotheisms and began to revive a Goddess religion which would meet their needs. Some of these women were attracted to Wicca, a process which was encouraged by the publication of the American Witch Starhawk's books, which made explicit the links between Wicca, the women's movement and ecology.

Goddess religion and women's spiritual groups are empowering for women because they demonstrate that the Divine is made in their image. They are not excluded from a full spiritual life or from the definition of what is ultimately spiritual. The Goddess is worshipped in women's groups as manifest in Nature, beyond Nature and also within each individual woman. Often ritual incorporates powerful self-affirmation and affirmation by others. These are valuable healing experiences for all women and especially those who have suffered in abusive relationships.

WICCA AND WISECRAFT

Wicca is the name often given to the religion of Witchcraft, also called the WiseCraft or, more simply, the Craft. It has been one of the most vigorous branches of the Pagan revival and is not just a form of magic, but a whole system of Pagan philosophy and religious belief. Witches worship the Divine as the Great Mother Goddess and her consort the Horned God, who appear in different aspects through the solar cycle of the seasons and throughout the monthly lunar cycle.

Many modern women (and men) believe that reclaiming the word 'Witch' is an important part of our Pagan heritage, a heritage which emphasizes our own inner strength and powers. The image of the Witch, which is closely aligned to that of the Shaman, offers women the possibility of harnessing this power and of using it in positive ways which benefit humankind – to heal and to change that which should be changed. The word 'Witch' is a difficult one, however, and to an outsider conveys something very different from its meaning within Paganism. It has not been easy for women to exercise their spiritual gifts in recent centuries and often those who did – the village midwives, herbalists and diviners – were condemned as Witches, as evil, as underminers of the male establishment. So, some Pagans prefer not to use the term. (Interestingly, the Black consciousness movement has gone through the same cycle of first reclaiming and rehabilitating a term used to derogate them by the dominant society – that of 'Black'. However, some people now prefer to term themselves 'People of Colour'.)

Wicca consists of a number of different traditions which are based on remnants of Pagan tradition which have been handed down through families. In the twentieth century, these traditions were in danger of dying out and a number of outsiders interested in Paganism became involved and took what could have been a dying set of beliefs and revived them in forms suitable for the coming millennium. In doing so, much was grafted onto the core of the folk traditions from elsewhere; principally from the various European Pagan traditions and from ritual magic, a magic which is dedicated to transformation of the self – the goal of the ancient Pagan mysteries, rather than spell craft. This has created a religion which encompasses a broad range of practice, from worshipping the Gods through the seasonal cycle to the development of psychic powers and the highest forms of mysticism.

Wicca has a very positive attitude towards women and they are essential in the priesthood. Since the Divine expresses Itself as female and male, Wicca believes that the Gods are best served by priestess and priest. Usually, the rites are performed jointly by a priestess and priest.

Wicca has no central authority structure, but consists of autonomous covens run by elders. There are also Witches who prefer to worship the Gods and practise their Craft alone.

DRUIDRY

Since the eighteenth century, Druidry has undergone an extensive revival all over the Western world, but particularly in England, Wales, France and North America. It is more structured than Wicca in that individual groups are usually part of Druid orders which are headed by a 'Chosen Chief', 'Archdruid' or similar head. Within Britain, most of the Druid orders belong to an umbrella body, the Council of British Druid Orders. This has not occurred in the United States, where the two main bodies are Ar nDraiocht Fein and Keltria.

Within the orders are three different grades: that of Bard, which focuses on the bardic arts, Ovate, in which divination is taught, and Druid, which is akin to the priesthood.

Modern Druids worship the ancient Celtic Deities and an attraction for many people, particularly those of Celtic ancestry, is Druidry's emphasis on the revival and transmission of Celtic culture, its focus on Nature worship and its encouragement of the creative arts of music, poetry and literature. Many people will be familiar with the large cultural gatherings such as the Welsh Eistedfodd. The Druids who organize these gatherings are not necessarily Pagans. Many Druid orders focus primarily on cultural revival and many have members who are Christian clergy. In this, Druidry has proved a useful meeting ground between Christian and Pagan.

Celtic spirituality's interpretation of Christianity is less hostile to Pagan thought than the Roman Catholic and Protestant varieties and shows a great continuity between Paganism and its Christian successor. The Celtic mind readily absorbed its Pagan Deities into the Christian framework as saints. Even animalistic Deities such as the Horned God, who was vilified by other branches of Christianity, found a home, reincarnated by the Celts of France as St Cornelly, patron saint of horned animals. The Catholicism of Celtic countries continues even today to honour its holy wells, formerly presided over by Pagan Goddesses, and Pagan prayers can be addressed to the Gods in their forms as Christian saints.

Druidry has also formed a useful bridge between Paganism and the wider community in that the holding of open seasonal festivals in public places has long been part of Druid tradition. Their public face has meant that Druids are better known than some of the other Pagan paths. In Britain, the most celebrated of these festivals was the Midsummer Solstice ceremony at dawn at Stonehenge. The story of Stonehenge illustrates how Paganism has grown.

When as a child I walked with my mother just before dawn to the mist-surrounded stones, we would pass a couple of tourist tents and wake up their occupants. At the site we would find the Druids themselves and maybe four or five other people. Fifteen or twenty of us at the most would celebrate the rising of the Sun. Then during the 1970s and 1980s, among younger people particularly, there was an awakening to Pagan heritage. Stonehenge became a great gathering place for those who wanted to meet together to celebrate life and the Gods and a free festival developed which proved many people's first encounter with Paganism. This event came to a sad end in 1985. After 30,000 people had gathered for the 1984 festival, the government decided to ban it. Undeterred, many people decided to try and reach Stonehenge for the 1985 Solstice. A huge police presence attacked those attempting the reach the site and one of the most shameful pieces of police oppression in recent British history followed – the Battle of the Beanfield. Aghast and disbelieving reporters and TV crews watched as the would-be festival-goers' vehicles were systematically destroyed and men, women and children attacked. Since then the Midsummer gatherings at Stonehenge have been banned, but Pagan organizations are still campaigning to reverse the decision.

THE NORTHERN TRADITION

The present day followers of the Northern European Pagan tradition are often called Odinists. Some prefer the term Asatru, which means 'belief in the Gods' or 'loyalty to the Aesir', as they do not worship solely Odin. Asatru is practised all over Northern Europe and also in North America. Like Druidry, it is organized into bodies with sub-groups, the hearths. There are two main Odinist organizations in Britain – the Odinshof and the Odinic Rite – and also in the United States – Arizona Kindred and the Asatru Free Assembly. In Iceland, Asatru is a strong religious movement and, with Christianity, is one of the two official state religions. Iceland only formally became Christian in 1000 CE and her Pagan religious history is therefore nearer to her people than in some of the other European countries.

Asatru is more male-oriented than some Pagan religions (although less so than Christianity), but Asatru groups are led by both men and women and both may officiate in religious ceremonies. Community priests are known as *Gothi* and may be men or women. Priestesses are also sometimes called *Volva*, which means 'prophetess'. Trance prophecy is under the patronage of the Goddess Freya and is considered to be primarily a female art.

Like the other Pagan paths, there is emphasis in Asatru on the sacredness of Nature. Asatru groups in Britain have taken a leading role in buying sacred woodland to reserve it for sacred use and in environmental campaigning.

MEN'S PAGANISM

Men's groups were slower to form in Paganism than women's groups but have developed with the growth of the men's movement as feminism has brought men to question their own role in society. Some groups have arisen from the work of Robert Bly and his book *Iron John* (Element Books, 1992), which has focused on the importance for men of initiation by other men into their societal role. This has meant exploring the male role through all-male gatherings which incorporate aspects of Shamanic practice and also the formation of more organized groups to explore the ancient male mystery traditions. These include the Mysteries of Orpheus and Mithras. Groups have also formed of gay men who prefer to honour their Gods together.

This then is a snapshot of the Pagan community. Who and what do they worship?

PAGAN DEITIES: BEAUTY IN DIVERSITY

Our ancestors honoured Nature in her many manifestations because they had a deep and intimate relationship with the natural landscape. It is easy to imagine how certain places came to be seen as sacred and how we came to worship the Deities of distinctive natural features such as rocks, trees, mountains, lakes, rivers or springs. Our original Gods belonged often to specific places.

Other Gods belonged to specific tribes. Nomadic peoples, who were hunters and later herders, needed portable Gods. Each tribe or clan had its own presiding Deity who guarded and protected his or her people. Examples of tribal Deities include Yahweh, who later became known as Jehovah, the God of the Israelites, and Dana, the Great Mother Goddess of the tribe known in Irish legend as the *Tuatha dé Danaan*, People of Dana.

The early needs of our ancestors were simple, so they did not have complex pantheons of Gods. As human society evolved, so too did our religious ideas. New mysterious skills were learned – the power to smelt metal, agriculture, the written word. In time, certain important human activities came to have their own presiding Deities who initiated their worshippers into the mysteries of their arts. Sometimes Deities had more than one function. Sometimes a function had more than one Deity. The Egyptian God Thoth or Tahuti was the patron of the Egyptian hieroglyphic script, but words were sacred, so he was also a patron of magic. The Goddess Isis was a patron of magic too, for it was she who persuaded her father the Sun God Ra to give her the secret of the word of power which would raise her husband Osiris from the dead. Sometimes a function in society would be ruled by a Goddess and sometimes by a God. In Greece, the God Hephaestos became the patron of smiths, whereas in Ireland this was mainly under the patronage of the Goddess Bride. Thus did the Gods and Goddesses multiply and our ancestors were polytheists – worshippers of many Deities.

Many Deities were forgotten. Others survived. The reasons are partly political and partly archaeological. We know the Roman Deities, for example, because the Romans were a powerful military people whose Empire spread across most of Europe and North Africa. They were also a literary people. We have written records and stone inscriptions on the monuments they left behind which tell us of their religious beliefs.

The Gods and Goddesses of the Celts are venerated particularly within Druidry and WiseCraft, but we know much less about them. The Celts did not record their names and believed religious teachings were too sacred to commit to writing. The Celtic Deities we do know are difficult to understand. To the Celts, like many Pagan peoples, the Divine and human worlds were not distinct. Gods could marry human beings and produce offspring and it is not always clear whether a hero figure or a queen is an historical personage, a mythological figure, human or Divine. Another difficulty is that religious myths were not written down until the Christian era. So sometimes Gods and Goddess were described as men and women to escape monastic censorship, as well as through lack of understanding.

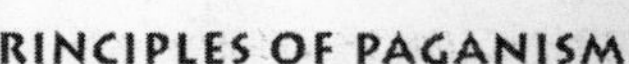

However, the attributes and magical powers of the figures in the legends betray their Divine origins.

The Deities of Northern Europe – the *Aesir* or High Gods, chief of whom is Odin, and the *Vanir* Deities, whose principal Deities are Freya and Frey – are venerated by those who follow the Northern Tradition and within Northern European Wicca. We have the same problems interpreting Northern European traditions as we do Celtic. This was also an oral society and very little was recorded of its religious myths until after the Christianization of Northern Europe from 1000 CE onwards when Christian scholars became concerned that their cultural heritage would be lost.

Other pantheons of Deities are known to us because their worshippers developed powerful and sophisticated forms of religion. The Gods and Goddesses of the ancient Egyptians were worshipped for thousands of years, not only in Egypt but also in Europe, and the accumulated energy of that worship gives their forms and images a strength and evocativeness which still speak to us today.

Although our ancestors were polytheists, with time some came to believe that some Deities who were called by different names by different peoples were the same or nearly the same. People's awareness of this grew with travel. We often think of our ancestors as narrow-visioned people who knew nothing of what lay beyond the boundaries of their own villages. This is not true. Many of our them lived in multi-cultural and multi-lingual societies. While many *were* tied to the land, the great force of commerce meant that there was a continual movement of peoples around their own known worlds.

In America, for example, there was huge trade between the Native American peoples across the divide we now call North and South America. In Europe, we find in France Egyptian beads brought by traders from North Africa. From the city of

Carthage on the north coast of Africa, Phoenician sailors set forth to trade tin with the Celts of Cornish Britain. Greeks travelled north to trade with Swedes and eastwards to India. These commercial links provided opportunities whereby not only material goods were exchanged but also ideas, intellectual discussion and knowledge of the Gods.

It was in encountering the Deities of others that travellers came to realize that although different peoples might depict their Gods in different ways, the archetypal ideas behind them were the same. Thus the ancient Greek traveller Herodotus could say that the Egyptians worship the Goddess of Love, whom we call Aphrodite, under the name of Bast. All this led to a religious tolerance and respect for other people's religious ideas. Athens even had a monument to the Unknown God, meaning that the city honoured those Deities who were not yet known to the citizens. This tolerance was to prove fatal when other more militant religions came to birth.

In time, another religious idea evolved naturally from the interaction between different peoples and their different Deities. This was that not only were the Goddesses of Love of different peoples different names for the same Goddess, but that all the different Goddesses who were worshipped were not entirely separate beings, but were different aspects of the one being – the Great Goddess. Thus in Egypt, Isis came in time to represent many different Goddesses. A similar process happened with the Gods. Beyond this, some of our Pagan ancestors came to believe that the Goddess and God themselves were manifestations of two different aspects of the One Divine being.

One logical extension of this was monotheism, which is practised today by Jews, Christians and Muslims. Here, people choose one particular Deity (usually a male God) and decide that this is the only true God. All other Deities are bad and evil. Paganism does not take this view, but rather considers that any

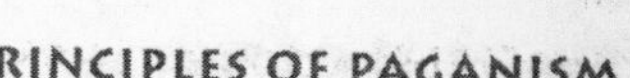

image of the Divine that our minds can form will be limited, for the complexity of the Divine cannot be captured by the words or pictures of the human mind. The different forms in which the Divine has chosen to manifest to us are necessary for us to understand Its variety and richness.

Why do we need to describe our Gods at all? Why do we not just say that the Divine is abstract? Unfortunately, the human mind, for most of us anyway, does not think in abstractions. Thus the beautiful forms of the Gods which our ancestors have worshipped over the ages still have the power to move us, inspire us, stretch our minds. We know that each image by itself is limited, but if we honour the many Gods in our minds, our hearts and our spirit, they will bring us to a true understanding: that the Divine is present within us and without us, in all times and places, ever-changing, ever the same.

MODERN PAGANISM AND ANCIENT GODS

Some modern Pagans have a devotion to a particular Goddess or God; others choose to venerate the Divine through the Gods and Goddesses of one particular pantheon. Often, however, Pagans honour the Gods under a number of different names. This can seem somewhat bewildering but it is perhaps less so if the Gods are thought of as different personalities through which the Divine has chosen to manifest Itself at different times and to different peoples.

Although modern Pagans worship the Gods using their ancient names, this does not mean that we think of our Gods in exactly the same way as ancient Pagans did. If a modern Irish woman chooses to call the Great Goddess Isis, this does not mean that her concept of Isis is exactly the same as that of an Egyptian woman 4,000 years ago. Over time, our ideas about the Gods and the nature of the Divine have changed. We are not seeking to restore our Paganism to exactly the same practices as those of our ancestors, even if this were possible. Much has been lost to us; much of our religious thinking has evolved. We must examine the ancient myths and legends in order to find a new way forward for the future. Paganism can be considered a lost knowledge which has now been rediscovered and must be reinterpreted in ways which meet the needs of people today.

Some aspects of our ancestors' Pagan practice would not find favour today. Like Judaism and other religions of the pre-Christian period, many types of Paganism practised animal sacrifice. This is not acceptable to modern Pagans and indeed there were many ancient Pagans who practised vegetarianism. Other ancient Pagan ideas would seem bizarre nowadays. Our ancestors thought it perfectly normal to honour a Deity, make requests and then to threaten to take their worship elsewhere if their requests were not carried out. When the Gods are seen as different personalities, it is logical for people to switch allegiance if they feel they can get a 'better deal' elsewhere – as indeed people did with Christianity. Modern Pagans would not consider this an appropriate way in which to treat their Gods.

Today, Pagans worship the Divine as Goddess, God and also as the Great Spirit or One who is beyond all these. Some Pagans honour the Gods in their Norse form, others in Celtic form, Egyptian form or according to the ways of Native American ancestors. A distinctive feature of Paganism, however, is the emphasis it places on the Divine in female form – the Goddess.

GODDESS

In whatever Pagan pantheon we look, we find strong and powerful Goddess figures, queens in their own right, Mistresses of the worlds of Magic, the Otherworld and the everyday world of women and men. Above all, we have in the Goddess the image of the loving mother, who provides for us, cherishes us, who gives us rest when we are weary, food when we are hungry, healing when we are in pain, hope in the darkest hour of the dawn of another day and, when the ravaging wolf attacks, she it is who with her last breath protects us. For most of us our mother is the first person whom we encounter when we enter the world. She cherishes us, feeds us, loves us. We are totally dependent on her. It is natural therefore for our first ideas of Deity to be female.

Many modern Pagans speak of 'The Goddess', meaning the essence behind all the different Goddesses who have been worshipped all over the world. A chant which is often heard at Pagan gatherings sings to the Goddess as:

Isis, Astarte, Diana, Hecate, Demeter, Kali, Inanna.

These many names from the past are seen as representing different aspects of the Great Goddess who is universal and present in all cultures and at all times, the eternal feminine, the Divine She.

Some branches of Paganism see Goddess and God as two aspects of the polarity found in energy – receptive and active, creative and destructive. This does not mean that the feminine aspect of the Divine is passive. Many Pagans have a similar view to Hindus, whereby all manifestation, whether of consciousness or matter, is symbolized by Shakti the Great Mother of All. Shakti is energy and power, but energy and power must take shape or form. This is Shiva the Great Father of All. This view is the opposite of that found in Judaic thought, which has in turn influenced Christian thinking. In Jewish mysticism, the Great Mother, Binah, is seen as the receptive womb which gives form to the force and energy emitted by the Father, Chokmah.

Women's Paganism and Wicca see the Goddess as the Creatrix. Rather than a notion of a creator God as architect of the universe, with the masculine being the primary force and the feminine arising from it, the Goddess is seen as the dynamic force which gives birth to the universe either by a process by which she calls the God to her or by parthogenesis (giving birth from herself alone – a virgin birth).

The emphasis on the Goddess varies between individuals and groups, but most Pagans believe that for wholeness the Divine must contain images of both female and male. An overemphasis on a masculine transcendent vision of Divinity during the past two millennia has led to social structures which glorify the masculine, the spiritual and the intellectual at the expense of the manifest universe and the realm of empathy and feeling. This has led to an exploitative attitude towards Nature and towards those who do not form part of the masculine power structure. For some Pagans, the solution, at least for the present time, is to focus on the Divine feminine as an antidote to over-masculinization. Other Pagans believe that a reaction in the opposite direction will not rebalance society but will encourage a polarization of values. They look to a balance between Goddess and God, feminine and masculine, both within themselves and in outer society, as the way forward.

In many cases, we know little of the Deities whose names are known to us and even with better known Deities we must make surmises based on archaeological and historical evidence and on what we know about mythology and the psychology of myth. So, a danger is that we project backwards onto history ideas that meet our needs in the present. In a sense, this is what has happened throughout history. Teasing out the web of cause and effect to determine the patterning of events is a difficult art. Each society has different preconceptions and these influence those aspects of history which they remember and record. Until recently, women's history was all but ignored and so too were the roles of Goddesses and queens.

Since the nineteenth century, both men and women have attempted to redress this balance and in doing so may have gone too far. Feminist history has popularized the idea of a matriarchal society which was entirely peaceful and which endured until the Neolithic peoples of the New Stone Age were overrun by male-dominated, metal-bearing, warrior peoples. In some regions, this may have been true, but we know that warfare was not entirely confined to the Bronze Age and onwards. Earlier settlements show evidence of defensive fortifications which would only have been necessary if warfare was a regular occurrence. We also do not know to what extent ancient societies were matrilinear or matriarchal. What we do know is that the Christian era brought about a disempowering of women and the appropriation to maleness of the nature of the Divine. What we find in Paganism are powerful Goddess figures who can have deep meaning for women and men today.

These are some Goddesses who are worshipped by modern Pagans.

THE TRIPLE GODDESS

One concept of the Goddess which is found in ancient Paganism but which is more widespread in modern Paganism is that of the Triple Goddess – the Goddess as a triplicity of Virgin, Mother and Crone, often symbolized by the Waxing, Full and Waning Moons. This image is found primarily in WiseCraft, women's groups and eclectic Paganism.

Why does the Triple Goddess have such modern appeal? The Gods and Goddesses whom we choose to worship do not influence only our spiritual lives. They also influence the social structures of the societies which worship them. One reason for the popularity of the Triple Goddess is that She represents all aspects of the female life-cycle – the freedom and independence of youth, the joys and the sorrows of motherhood, and the wisdom and independence which return when we are free of the obligations of family. Modern society has tended to venerate the young and the beautiful and to neglect and devalue other aspects of womanhood. An image of Deity in which age is as important as youth is empowering for women and instructive for men.

Another important aspect of the Triple Goddess is that She is both sexual and a mother. Bizarrely, these two aspects have been divorced in the nearest recent Western equivalent to the Goddess – the Virgin Mary of the Catholics. This leads to a denigration of the life of the body which can be damaging for both women and men. In Paganism the Virgin aspect of the Goddess is not necessarily Virgin in the sense of non-sexual, but Virgin in the sense of not owned by a husband.

The Mother aspect of the Triple Goddess is represented by the Full Moon. She is also represented by the Earth. Often this aspect of the Goddess is seen as Gaia, the Earth itself, and is thought of as The Great Mother – the Divinity which gives birth to us, nourishes us, sustains us, and in which we finally find our rest and rebirth. This aspect of the Goddess, although suppressed by the Christian Church, persisted throughout the medieval period amongst scholars and others who were still oriented to the ways of ancient Paganism. In a twelfth-century English herbal, for instance, the Goddess is hymned as:

Earth, Divine Goddess, Mother Nature,
who dost generate all things
and bringest forth ever anew the Sun
which Thou hast given to the nation;
Guardian of sky and sea and of all Gods and powers;
through Thy influence all Nature is hushed and sinks to sleep...
Again, when it pleases Thee,
Thou sendest forth the glad daylight
and nurturest life with Thine eternal surety;
and when the spirit of humankind passes,
to Thee it returns.
Thou indeed art rightly named Great Mother of the Gods;
Victory is Thy Divine name.
Thou art the source of the strength of peoples and Gods;
without Thee nothing can either be born or made perfect;
Thou art mighty, Queen of the Gods.
Goddess, I adore Thee as Divine,
I invoke Thy name;
vouchsafe to grant that which I ask of Thee,
so shall I in return give thanks to Thy Godhead,
with the faith that is Thy due.

The Triple Goddess is also honoured as Wise Woman, Crone or Hag, the keeper of the mysteries. For a woman, the Crone Goddess symbolizes her own inner wisdom, but also the female elders who in a tribal society would have taught her what she needed to know about her womanhood. In older societies, the elders were the living repositories of the history and lore of the tribe. They were its libraries, reference point, databank. Their role was essential to the successful functioning of society and age had an honoured place.

VIRGIN GODDESSES: DIANA AND ARADIA

Two Roman Goddesses who play an important role in women's Paganism and in WiseCraft are the Moon Goddess Diana and her daughter Aradia. One particular branch of WiseCraft – the Dianic Craft, which is primarily for women – is dedicated to Diana. Despite her role as Virgin Goddess, Diana presided over childbirth and could bless women with children. She seems her therefore not to be Virgin in the sense of non-sexual, but Virgin in the sense of non-married.

Aradia is the Italian version of the name of the Classical Goddess Herodias, whom some medieval texts claim was widely worshipped across Southern Europe into medieval times. The name came into English usage via the nineteenth-century collection of the lore and legends of Tuscany called *Aradia: The Gospel of the Witches*.

Aradia and her mother Diana are described as saviour Goddesses of the peasants against their oppressive feudal lords. Diana could be appealed to for help in all of life's problems because, *Aradia: Gospel of the Witches* tells us:

Diana hath the power to do all things,
to give glory to the lowly,
wealth to the poor,
joy to the afflicted,
beauty to the ugly.
Be not in grief, if you are her followers;
though you be in prison and in darkness,
she will bring light...

MOTHER GODDESS: ISIS

Isis is an Egyptian Mother Goddess who was widely worshipped throughout Egyptian history. She was the sister of Osiris, the God of Death and Resurrection, and mother of the God Horus. One of the largest Goddess-worshipping movements in the Western world today is the Fellowship of Isis.

Isis became widely known following Alexander the Great's conquest of Egypt about 2,000 years ago. Greek followers of Alexander took over as rulers of Egypt and were anxious to integrate themselves with Egyptian society. To provide a unifying religion, a small number of Deities were 'promoted' to being chief Gods of Egypt and a focus of worship for Egyptian and Greek alike. The most popular Deity was Isis.

Then the Romans, finding the religions offered by the state unsatisfying, looked elsewhere. They were as fascinated with the East as the many spiritual seekers who headed East in the nineteenth and twentieth centuries, so by the time of Julius Caesar, a temple of Isis had been established in Rome on the Capitoline Hill. It lasted for four centuries. For many, Isis became *the* Goddess. A hymn to her from the first century BCE says:

All mortals dwelling on the infinite earth –
Thracians, Greeks, even Barbarians –
pronounce Thy blessèd name, honoured by all;
each in his own tongue and in his own land.
The Syrians address Thee as Astarte,
as Nanaia, or as Artemis.
Thy Lycian worshippers call thee Leto,
the people of Thrace – Great Mother of the Gods.
In Greece they call Thee Hera, throned on high,
or Aphrodite, or well-wishing Hestia,
Rhea or Demeter too.

But the Egyptians name Thee Thioui,
for Thou and Thou alone art all the Goddesses
which different people call by different names.

CRONE GODDESSES: HECATE, MORRIGAN, CERRIDWEN

HECATE

The Crone aspect of the Goddess is often venerated in the form of Hecate, a Greek Moon Goddess and Goddess of Witchery. She is worshipped both in WiseCraft and by women's groups.

The Greek Moon Goddesses were originally three – Artemis of the Waxing Virgin Moon, Selene of the Full Moon and Hecate of the Waning Moon. Later statues of Hecate show her as three Goddesses facing in different directions – a Triple Goddess representing all aspects of the Moon. These statues may also represent her power in the Heavens, on Earth and in the Underworld.

Hecate was called Antea, sender of nocturnal visions, and her rites were often performed at night – as is fitting for a Moon Goddess. She was particularly associated with cross-roads, which have always been thought of as places of change and transformation.

In Greece her main festival was at the August harvest – the equivalent of the Lammas harvest celebration in Western Paganism. Hecate was associated with the Moon and the Moon with rain, for the weather often changes at the New and Full Moons. She was therefore seen as having control over the weather and her aid was invoked to help avert storms which might damage the August harvest.

MORRIGAN

The Morrigan is venerated in Celtic traditions of WiseCraft and

in Druidry. In Celtic mythology, she is the fearsome and powerful Triple Goddess of Battle and Death, who appears in her three forms of Morrigan, Badhbh and Nemhain. Her symbol is the raven, which is perhaps not surprising, given that ravens feast on the bodies of the dead after battle.

In modern Paganism, Morrigan is often closely associated with Hecate.

CERRIDWEN

Another Celtic Deity whose name is widely used in Druidry and WiseCraft is the Welsh Goddess Cerridwen. There are few mentions of her in the Welsh texts, but she was nevertheless widely invoked by the Welsh medieval bards and thence by the eighteenth-century restorers of the Druidic traditions. Her legend is as follows.

Cerridwen lives on an island in Lake Tegid with her husband Tegid Foel by whom she has two children – a beautiful daughter Creirwy and an ugly son Afagddu. To compensate for her son's ugliness, she determines to make him the wisest in the land. For a whole year she prepares a magic brew in her Cauldron of Inspiration, adding throughout the year magical herbs gathered at the correct planetary hours.

However, her plans go awry. When the brew is ready three drops fall accidentally on the fingers of a young boy, Gwion Bach, who has been charged with supplying wood for the fire which heats the cauldron. Gwion thrusts his burned fingers into his mouth and tastes the magical drops, thus appropriating the wisdom which has been brewed for Afagddu. He takes flight and Cerridwen pursues him in revenge. To escape her, Gwion uses the magical powers he has gained to turn himself into a hare, but Cerridwen transforms herself into a greyhound and is hot on his heels. Gwion plunges into a river and turns himself into a fish. Cerridwen pursues as an otter. He flies into the air as a bird. She becomes a hawk. He becomes a grain of wheat on a barn floor and she becomes a hen and eats him.

This does not put an end to Gwion. When Cerridwen transforms herself back into her own form, she finds herself pregnant with Gwion. Nine months later she bears him and intends to kill him, but he is so beautiful that she cannot. Instead, she places him in a leather bag and casts him out to sea. He floats for two days and on Beltane is rescued from a salmon weir by Elphin, a nephew of the King of North Wales, who names him Taliesin, 'Shining Brow'.

The salmon is significant because this was considered a symbol of knowledge and wisdom in Celtic tradition. With its seemingly magical ability to go out to sea and then find its way back upriver, leaping up waterfalls if necessary, to its spawning grounds each year, it was a fitting symbol of hidden knowledge.

In modern Paganism, Cerridwen is often associated with Hecate. Both are Goddesses associated with magic and Cerridwen, like Hecate, is associated with the Crone aspect of the Goddess, the Waning Moon. A popular Goddess chant is:

Hecate, Cerridwen, Dark Mother, take us in
Hecate, Cerridwen, let us be reborn.

Why should there be so much interest in these superficially less attractive aspects of the Goddess?

Cerridwen is a Goddess of transformation and hence initiation. Many people coming to Paganism today are seeking inner wisdom and transformation, teachings which were once the province of the ancient Pagan mystery schools. Cerridwen is also is the keeper of hidden wisdom and although fearsome as Hag and pursuer, yet offers those who walk her ways insight into the depths of their soul and being.

STAR GODDESS: ARIANRHOD

Arianrhod is another Welsh Goddess and is invoked often in WiseCraft and Druidry. Her names means 'Silver Wheel' and she is the mother of Lleu Llaw Gyffes, the Welsh equivalent of the Irish God Lugh. A chant to her is:

Arianrhod, Arianrhod,
Silver-Wheel, Silver-Wheel,
Crown of Stars, shining still.

Caer Arianrhod, the Castle of Arianrhod, is placed in the Northern heavens and Arianrhod is associated with the pole-star. Caer Arianrhod is considered particularly sacred in some traditions of WiseCraft as the shining beacon which guides our spiritual destiny.

FIRE GODDESS: BRIDE

The Irish Goddess Brigit, Brigid or Bride (pronounced *Breed*), patron of artists, smiths and healers, is honoured in Druidry and WiseCraft. Bride was the daughter of the *Dagda* or Good God, the principal God of the Irish race known as the *Tuatha dé Danaan*, People of Dana, Dana being the Mother Goddess.

Brigit was often depicted as a Triple Goddess. Her chief shrine was in Kildare, where her vigil fire was tended by unmarried priestesses known as *Inghean an Dagha*, Daughters of Fire. With the Christianization of Ireland, Brigid became St Brigid and her shrine was taken over by nuns. Legend tells us that the nuns continued to tend her sacred flame until the thirteenth century, when the Bishop of Kildare decreed that the custom was Pagan and must cease. However, Brigid remained a very popular saint in Ireland and Scotland until recent times and her importance rivalled that of the Virgin Mary.

RHIANNON

In Welsh myth, one of the most important Goddesses is Rhiannon. Scholars have suggested that her name means 'Great Queen'. Some believe she is the same horse Goddess who was venerated on Continental Europe as Epona. Epona was hailed as *Regina*, Queen, by her Roman followers and was worshipped by Celt and Roman alike during the time of the Roman Empire.

Rhiannon is married to Pwyll, Lord of Llys Arberth, who later became known as Lord of the Otherworld. Pwyll first encounters Rhiannon at Gorsedd Arberth when he sees her riding by dressed in gold and on a great white horse. He pursues her, but however fast he rides he cannot catch up with her. It is only when in desperation he pleads with her to stop and speak with him that she halts and decides to marry him in preference to her suitor Gwal.

FREYA

Freya is honoured today by Pagans of the Northern Tradition and also in Northern European Wicca. To our Northern ancestors, she was the most important Goddess of the Vanir Deities.

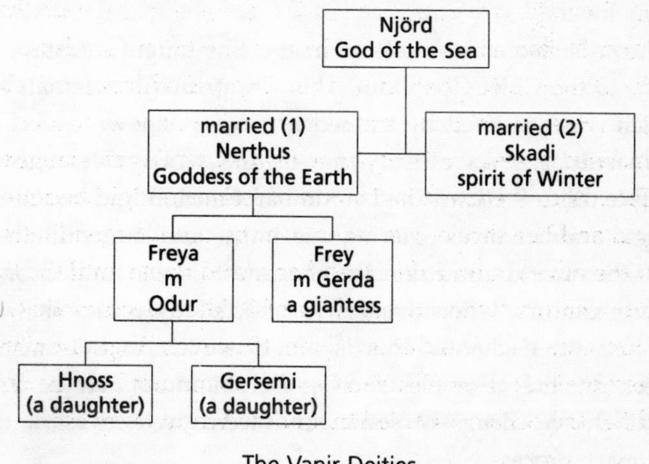

The Vanir Deities.

Medieval Icelandic scholar Snorri Sturloson, who recorded much of what we know today about the religion of Northern Europe, tells us that Freya was the most renowned of Goddesses. She and Odin are the most frequently mentioned Deities in German medieval texts.

Freya is a Goddess of Love, Beauty and Fertility, but half of the battle-slain are also hers. Riding across the battlefields with the Valkyrie warrior women, she makes her choice. Those who do not go to Freya's feasting hall go to that of Odin. Freya is married to Odur, whose name is so similar to that of Odin that many consider Freya and Frigga, Odin's wife, to be the same Goddess.

One story of Freya is of her journey in her chariot drawn by cats to search for her husband who has gone missing. Along the way, she weeps tears which turn into droplets of gold or droplets of amber, a stone long associated with the Goddess. It is said to be because of Freya's journey that amber is so widespread in Northern Europe. The myths do not tell us why Odur goes missing, but his and Freya's is not a monogamous relationship, as she was often taunted for her readiness to take many lovers.

Freya is also a patroness of magic. She taught seership, or *Seidr*, to the Chief God Odin. This was primarily a female art which was practised by trained priestesses known as *Volvas* and *Seidkonas*. As already noted, the word *Volva* means 'prophetess'. *Seidkonas* had a similar function and practised magic. *Seidr* involves entering into trance and journeying into the Otherworld. Traditionally, the priestess was seated on a high chair or platform and was assisted by a chorus who intoned ritual chants. This is not dissimilar to the ancient Greek practice at oracles such as Delphi and it may be that, as at Delphi, drugs of some kind were used to assist the visionary process.

FRIGGA

Frigga is the Mother of the Gods and Goddess of the Sky. She has the power to see the future and *knows every being's fate, though she herself says naught*. She is a patroness of marriage and fertility and seems to be much more chaste than Freya. Her health was always toasted at wedding feasts. She was also called upon by women in labour. Her hall was Fensalir where wives and husbands who had been faithful to one another would come after death. In her halls, she sat spinning golden threads and the constellation of Orion's Belt was known as Frigga's Spinning-Wheel.

Despite her domestic traits, Frigga's imagery is bound up with that of the medieval witch. A picture of Frigga naked riding a distaff which looks much like a broomstick can be found on the wall of Schleswig cathedral in North Germany. This image is from the twelfth century, which suggests that at that period Goddess worship had not succumbed entirely to Christianity.

GOD

Modern Paganism has many Gods, who, like its Goddesses, are drawn from a number of different pantheons. Many people come to Paganism seeking the Goddess and reverence for the God may come later, or they may prefer to focus their spirituality solely on the Goddess. The beauty of Paganism is that, like Hinduism but unlike the religions which have dominated the West in recent centuries, there is scope for each of us to develop a personal spirituality which meets our needs. There is room too for this to evolve. As we enter through our spiritual practice into a closer relationship with the Divine, our understanding may deepen and change. At one phase in our lives we may need to focus on the mysteries of the God, in another on the

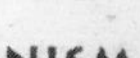

mysteries of the Goddess – or perhaps the lessons we need to learn are better expressed through one particular pantheon of Deities. This we can do, for the Gods of Paganism are not jealous Gods.

The Pagan God images differ from those of monotheisms in a number of significant ways. In Paganism, the God is conceived of as operating within Nature. The God is God of Fertility. Lord of the herds, the animals answer to His call; to Him we turn when we must hunt for food. He is a Father God, loving and protective, He cherishes His children; He guards the land when the cold winter comes; fierce He is in battle and in protecting the weak, the tired and those who bear burdens. The God is old, but young; strong and steadfast; light, energy, movement, creativity. Pagan God images are both animalistic and sexual. They recognize human beings in totality – that is, that we are creatures of primitive biological instinct, of human love and caring, and of spiritual longings and aspirations.

As with the Goddess, particular aspects of the Pagan Gods have risen to prominence in modern Paganism in order to meet the needs of Pagans today. Two of the most common aspects of the God are the Horned God and the Green Man. These aspects of Deity reflect modern Paganism's concern with maintaining our planet and our natural environment. The images of Divine as part of Nature which are conveyed by the Horned God and the Green Man are an important part of this process. They are also a recognition that we can live fulfilled and whole lives only if we acknowledge ourselves as part of Nature, not separate from it.

THE HORNED GOD

The Horned and phallic God is an image found in many Pagan cultures. As Pan he was venerated by the Greeks and as Faunus by the Romans. To the Egyptians he was the phallic (though

unhorned) Bes the dwarf God who was invoked to assist with childbirth and was also a patron of music and dance. To the Celts he was Cernunnos or Herne, names which derive from the word 'horn'.

Cernunnos' sacred animal is the stag and it is primarily as Stag God that the Horned God is honoured by Pagans today. His body is that of a man, but his feet are hooves and his antlers reach up to heaven, capturing within them the power of the Sun. The Pagan image of the Horned God has been much maligned in recent centuries by attempts to identify him with the Christian Devil, but modern Paganism has seen its rebirth and rehabilitation.

Why should this seemingly primitive and animalistic image hold such appeal? Many people who turn to Paganism believe that the cerebral and celibate images of God which have prevailed in recent millennia are negative for both women and men. The Christian God is a desexualized God, which creates problems in accommodating our sexual nature. Although he has a son, this son is born not from sex between father and mother. Instead the mother is visited by a spiritual essence and, although a mother, remains physically a virgin. The implicit message – and often the explicit one – is that sexuality is wrong.

So a man both desires women and feels guilty about it. Often the result is a fear of or repulsion towards women. The misogyny of recent history has been fostered by such thinking.

THE GREEN MAN

The Green Man is a very early form of Deity. Often he is found in conjunction with the Great Mother Goddess. He is both her son and her lover. She gives birth to him; he impregnates her; she sacrifices him and he is reborn. This was a way in which some of our ancestors symbolized the reappearance of green growth each spring and its disappearance in the autumn or fall.

The Green Man represents the return of fertility to the land after winter's bareness. He is therefore a phallic aspect of the God and a giver of plenty. In Babylonian mythology, he is associated with Tammuz, the son-lover of the Goddess Ishtar. Egyptian Osiris with his green face was also such a vegetation God who, with his capacity to resurrect, was also seen as Lord of the Otherworld. Much of the mythos of the Near Eastern vegetation Gods was grafted onto Christian legends of the dying and resurrecting God.

In English folklore celebrations, the Green Man appears as a tall man dressed in leaves and carrying a staff. Many Pagans believe that the English stories of Robin Hood, Maid Marian and their band of male followers in Sherwood Forest who protected the peasants against rapacious Christian clerics and feudal overlords originated in Pagan myths of the Green Man of the forest who wandered the woods accompanied by the Goddess, guarding and cherishing the life there.

DAGDA

Aspects of the Green Man are found in the Irish God, the Dagda. The Dagda is the All-Father, *Eochaid Ollathair*, and is wise and knowledgeable. His weapon is a club and he also possesses a magical cauldron which can never be emptied. There are suggestions that chalk image of a giant phallic figure with a staff which is carved into the hillside at the village of Cerne (i.e. horn) Abbas in South West England is an image of the Dagda or his English equivalent.

FREY

In the Northern Tradition, there are aspects of both the Green Man and the Horned God in Frey, the chief God of the Vanir, whose name means 'Lord'. Frey and his twin sister the Goddess Freya are the children of the fertility Earth Goddess Nerthus and the Sea God Njörd. Frey is distinguished by his erect phallus and has similarities to other Nature Gods such as Cernunnos and Pan. The link with the Horned God is appears when Frey fights Surt the destroyer with a pair of antlers, having given up his magical sword as part of a bride price.

THOR

Some aspects of the fertile, life-loving, Green Man aspect of the God are also found in the Northern Tradition in the form of the

red-bearded God Thor, or Thunor in Anglo-Saxon, whose name was given to Thursday. Thor is associated with oak trees and we know that the German tribes most frequently worshipped their Gods in forest clearings. Thor was a 'people's God' and his concerns were agriculture as well as war.

Thor was described as Odin's son by the giantess Jord or Jorth, who represents the Earth. He has earthy characteristics. He travels in a chariot drawn by goats. He has a zest for life and an enormous appetite for food and drink. He can literally drink his hosts dry.

Thor shares the Dagda's strength but his weapon is a hammer, Mjolnir, which can slay giants and shatter rocks, rather than a club. The Romans associated Thor with Hercules, another mighty wielder of clubs.

Thor is by no means purely, or even primarily, a Green Man. He is also a God of Lightning and was seen by the Romans as having many similarities to the Sky God Jupiter, to whom the oak was also sacred.

Together with Odin and Freya, Thor was one of the most widely worshipped of the Northern Gods. His popularity is evidenced by the frequency with which the image of Thor's hammer appears. The sign of the hammer was used to mark boundary stones. It was made over newborn children and was also marked on memorial stones for the dead. In the form of Thunor, this God was one of the three Deities the Saxons had to renounce when they converted to Christianity.

ODIN

Another major form in which the God is worshipped in modern Paganism is as Odin, who is also known by his Anglo-Saxon name of Woden or Wotan. Wednesday in the English calendar was originally Wotan's Day. This day is known in French and other Latin-based languages as Mercury's Day and Odin shares some of the same characteristics as the Roman Mercury. Both were depicted as wearing cloaks and wide-brimmed hats. Both have great wisdom, but also trickery. However, Odin is generally seen as an old man and Mercury as a youth. Odin is *Alfadhir*, the All-Father. These are some of his many relationships with the other Gods of Asgard, the home of the Aesir or High Gods:

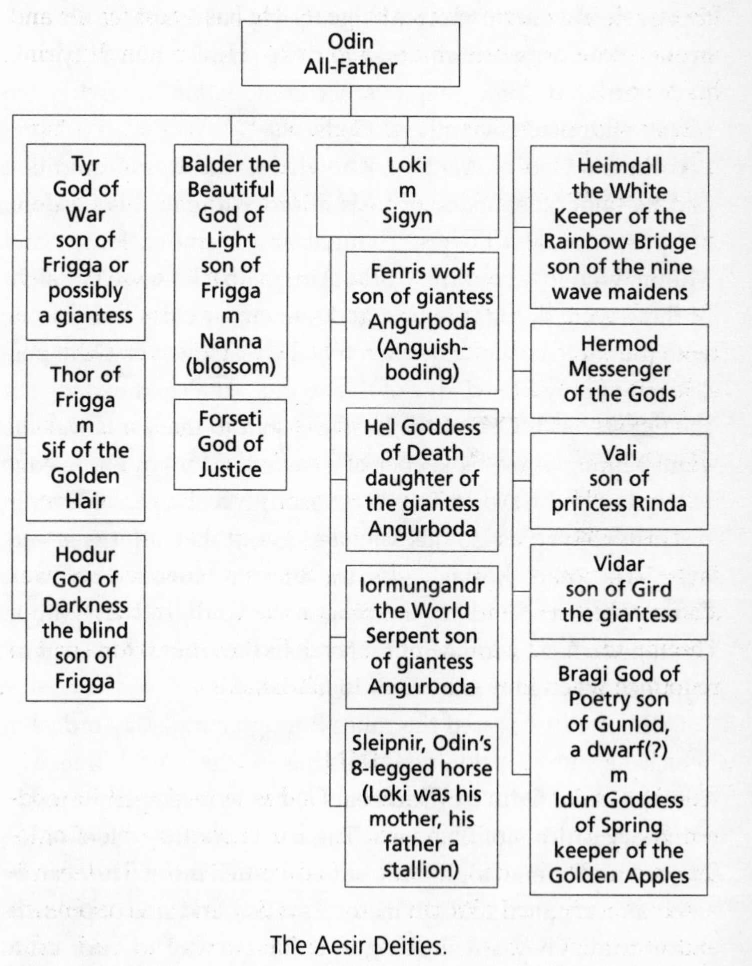

The Aesir Deities.

Many scholars believe that the Vanir were the Gods of the Bronze Age, whose followers came into conflict with the invading Iron Age Indo-Europeans and their warrior Aesir Gods. The myths describe how a war was fought between the two pantheons and was resolved when they exchanged hostages. Freya and her father Njörd were sent to make their home in Asgard and the Aesir sent two hostages to the Vanir. The custom of exchanging important hostages to ensure peace was not broken was common amongst ancient peoples and may well have reflected some religious accommodation whereby two peoples adopted each others' Gods.

Odin is a God of Wisdom, Knowledge and Communication and he undergoes many ordeals in order to gain his wisdom. He possesses two ravens, Thought and Memory, Hugin and Munin, who fly about the world bringing back news. The sight of these were thought to be a good omen for Odin's followers, who fought in battle under raven banners. However, Odin possesses not only knowledge of this world but also knowledge of the Otherworld. One of the hostages sent to the Vanir was the giant Mimir, who was keeper of a sacred spring of knowledge at the root of the World Tree. Odin sacrificed an eye to Mimir in order to gain access to this knowledge and thereafter was one-eyed. The other hostage was the unwise Hoenir. The Vanir found Hoenir could do nothing unless advised by Mimir. Outraged, they cut off Mimir's head and returned it to Asgard, where Odin used it to learn hidden lore.

Odin also discovered the runes through a nine day ordeal in which he hung upside-down fasting on the World Tree. The description of Odin's ordeal bears a strong resemblance to the initiatory ordeals of Shamans. The runes are the letters of the Norse and German alphabets, but also much more. They can be used as a magical and divinatory system and are popular as such today. They are shuffled in a similar way to tarot cards and the yarrow stalks of the *I Ching* and the pattern into which they fall is a microcosm – a miniature reflection – of the patterning of events in the universe. The right chanting of the runes can also be used as a method of magic-making and it certainly makes the hairs stand up on the back of the neck when it is heard. There are specific runes to help women in childbirth, to raise storms and to put enemies to flight.

Odin also possesses a magical ring which dispenses eight more like itself every ninth night. This was the inspiration for the rings in Tolkien's *Lord of the Rings*. Odin also had an eight-legged magical horse Sleipnir. Eight-legged horses have Shamanic associations and are known in Siberia as the horses on which Shamans ride between the worlds.

The Horned God venerated in WiseCraft shares some of the characteristics of Odin. In England, Herne is both Stag God and Leader of the Wild Hunt, but the original leader of the Wild Hunt was Odin and the concept is Germanic rather than Celtic.

There is a strong association between the English royal family and the Wild Hunt. The Wild Hunt is said to appear in the grounds of one of their principal residences, Windsor Castle, at times when England is in danger. There is also another royal tie-in with Odin. The Anglo-Saxon kings, from whom the current royal family are directly descended, claimed their royal lineage and descent from Wotan. The English royal family can therefore be said to be descended directly from Odin or Woden/Wotan.

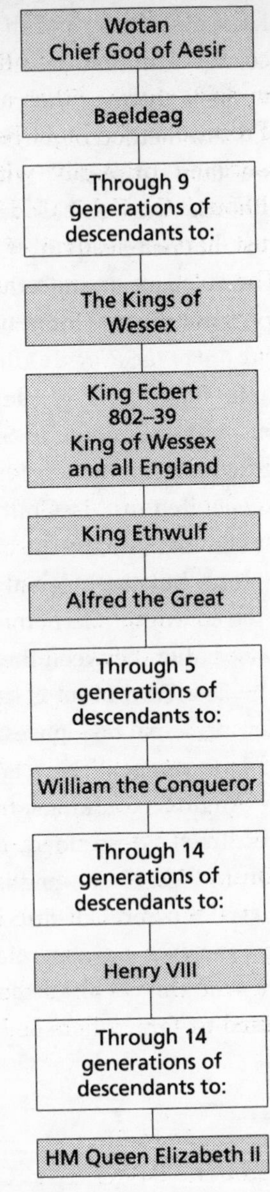

Descent of the English monarch from the God Wotan (Odin).

GODS OF LIGHT

In the Pagan calendar, there are many festivals when the God appears primarily in solar guise, either as a Sun King, Sun Child, the Child of Promise or the Light Bearer. These aspects of the God are associated primarily with the Winter and Summer Solstices, although the Celtic God Lugh is also associated with the August harvest festival of Lughnasadh (pronounced *Loonasa*). The solstices are natural times at which to think of the Sun, for we notice something most when it is very present or very absent.

LUGH

Lugh is an Irish Deity, the grandson of the healing God Dian Cécht. He comes to the Hall of the High King of Ireland in Tara at the head of what is described in the Irish text as an 'extraordinary troop'. Lugh is described as a young warrior of fair countenance, equipped like a king. He demands admission and is told that no one can enter unless they have a useful skill. Lugh then claims to be able to do most of the recognized occupations in roughly ascending order of prestige. First he claims to be a carpenter, but that is not considered sufficient because Tara already has a carpenter. He then claims to be a smith, champion, harper, hero, historian, magician, doctor and poet. None of these will suffice. He then announces himself as the more lowly 'artisan' and, when this is still insufficient to gain entry, he asks, perhaps somewhat exasperatedly, whether there is anyone else in Tara who can do all of these things. There is not. So Lugh is admitted to Tara, where he becomes adviser to the king.

BALDER

In the Northern Tradition, Balder is a God of Light and Radiance, whose brother is blind Hodur, the darkness. Balder and Hodur are the sons of Frigga and Odin. Odin engraves the runes upon Balder's tongue which gives him the power to sing the runes and so to perform magic. He is so beautiful and good that his appearance fills everyone with gladness. He lives in a sacred hall into which nothing unclean may enter. Its walls are of gold and its roof of silver. Balder is married to Nanna, whose name means 'blossom'. He is almost immortal, for there is only one thing in existence which can harm him: mistletoe.

There are some interesting parallels between the story of Balder and Celtic myth. The equivalent of Lugh in Welsh myth is Lleu Llaw Gyffes, 'Bright One of the Skilful Hand'. His mother Arianrhod has placed a curse on him that no one shall name him unless she agrees, that he shall bear no arms unless she gives them to him and that he shall have no mortal wife. Without name, arms or a wife, he can never become adult. As with Balder, Lleu is supernaturally protected from death in that he cannot be killed indoors or out, on land or on water, naked or clothed, only by a spear made at a time when such work is forbidden. The magician Gwydion helps Lleu overcome his mother's curses and conjures for him a wife of flowers, Blodeuwedd, whose name echoes that of Nanna (Blossom), the wife of Balder.

In both cases an enemy conspires to discover how the God's supernatural protection can be overcome and the God killed. In the case of Balder it is half-brother Loki, known as the Wizard of Lies, who brings about his downfall. In the Welsh myth, it is Blodeuwedd. Lleu reveals his only point of vulnerability to her and dies by a spear at the hands of Blodeuwedd's lover. Balder is killed when Loki tricks their mother Frigga into revealing that mistletoe can kill him. At Midwinter Solstice, Loki fashions a mistletoe dart and tricks Balder's brother, the blind Holdur, into throwing it. Balder is killed. He is not reborn because Loki conspires to prevent it, but Lleu is saved. When the spear enters him, he turns into an eagle and is eventually rescued and returned to his own form.

These are by no means all of the many different forms in which modern Pagans honour their Gods, but those described here will give a glimpse of the richness of Pagan mythology and also how it is being reinterpreted to meet the needs of Pagans today. In the next chapter we will look at Pagan festivals and see how the different aspects of the Deities are honoured at different points of the seasonal cycle.

PAGAN FESTIVALS

All religions have seasonal festivals which mark the calendar of the year. In countries where Christianity has been the dominant religion, public holidays centre around Christian festivals. These tell the life story of one man who is considered an incarnate God and also the lives of holy men and women – saints. Many of the ideas and symbolism used have been borrowed from pre-Christian Paganism. This is particularly noticeable in countries which have been dominated by the Catholic version of Christianity.

Most Pagans celebrate a seasonal cycle of eight festivals. Four of these are known by their Celtic names. The other four are related to the solar cycle – the Spring and Autumn or Fall Equinoxes, when the hours of daylight equal the hours of light; Summer Solstice, the longest day; and Winter Solstice, the longest night of the year. These eight festivals are spaced throughout the year, so there is a Pagan festival every six to seven weeks. The seasonal cycle is often called the Wheel of the Year.

Below are the dates of the major festivals in the Northern Hemisphere.

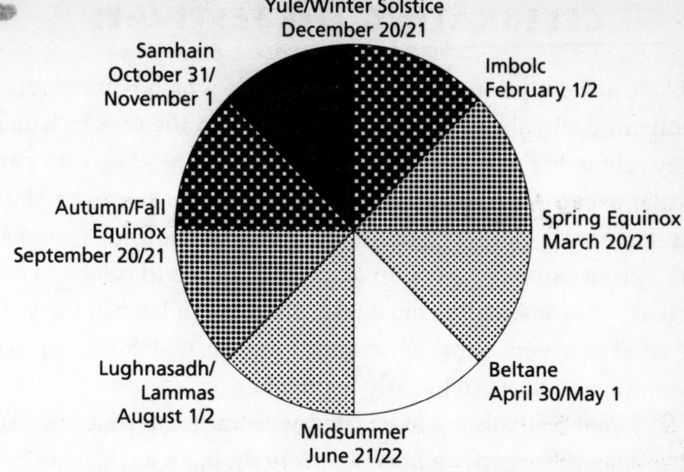

The Wheel of the Year in the Northern Hemisphere

These dates refer to the Northern Hemisphere of the world only. In Australia and New Zealand, the longest day is on 20/21 December and the cycle must be adjusted accordingly.

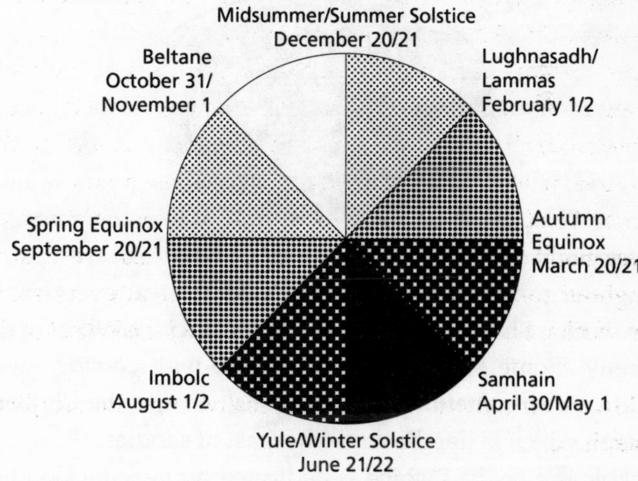

The Wheel of the Year in the Southern Hemisphere.

This is a description of the seasonal cycle which is based on a temperate climate. Pagans, however, vary in the way in which they celebrate the festivals and the emphasis they place on particular aspects of each festival. Some variations are regional. In the far North, parts of Scandinavia and Canada for instance, the Spring Equinox is not an appropriate time to celebrate the sowing of seeds, as this must take place much later in the year in what is a very short agricultural season which takes place from the end of April to early September.

Different festivals are associated with different times of day. This does not mean we have to celebrate them at those times, but meditating on the symbolism of the timing will help us to understand the meaning of the festival.

IMBOLC/CANDLEMAS (THE HOURS BEFORE AND UP TO DAWN)

Life is renewing, the light is returning.

Imbolc is an Irish word and originally it was thought to mean 'in the belly'. Some Pagans also associate it with *Oi-melc*, ewe's milk. It is also sometimes known by its name in the Christian calendar, which is Candlemas – the feast of candles.

Imbolc is a festival which is dedicated both to the Goddess and to the return of light to the land. In many Pagan traditions, the Goddess is considered to be in the Underworld throughout the winter. The land is barren, there is no sign of the Goddess' green cloak. All is hidden beneath winter snows. Around Imbolc, the first signs of the passing of winter appear. Although the days lengthen after the Winter Solstice, the increased daylight is only at the end of the day. For many mornings dawn is still a little later each day. By Imbolc, however, there is a noticeable difference. We are confident that the Sun is returning.

The lengthening days awaken Nature. The first spring flowers appear – snowdrops, crocuses – sometimes emerging from the snow itself. We know that even if the land seems barren, the life force is awakening and will renew itself once more.

Our ancestors celebrated this festival with light. In Scandinavia, a young woman representing the Goddess was crowned with a crown of candles. In Northern countries people would go out with torchlit processions to celebrate with fire the return of the Sun. This was also a time when in countries which practised sheep farming new lambs would be born – hence the reference to ewe's milk.

Pagans today celebrate Imbolc in many ways. The Goddess may be invited to leave the Underworld and to return to the Middle World, the world of Nature. She can be invited by an invocation – a calling unto the Goddess. This might be by one person or by many. It could be a beautiful piece of ritual poetry or prose, or a song or chant, perhaps using Goddess names appropriate to the time of year. It could be a silent call by a solitary Pagan who lights a single candle or a chant and dance with wild drumming by a group all calling upon the Goddess.

One Goddess who is frequently invoked at Imbolc is the Celtic Goddess Brigid or Bride. As a Fire Goddess, she is appropriate to a festival which celebrates the return of the Sun and longer days. Bride is not considered a married Goddess, but virgin. Fire Goddesses served by unmarried women were found often in Pagan society. In ancient Rome, the Goddess Vesta was the Fire Goddess and she was served by specially selected noblewomen who were known as Vestal Virgins. These women had great power and influence.

In modern Pagan celebration, a young woman may be chosen to represent Bride. She will emerge out of the darkness wearing a crown of candles over a white veil to symbolize her purity. She will be welcomed with the words: 'Bride is Welcome! Bride is come!' This image of Bride is still found in modern secular society in the bride dressed in white and crowned with flowers.

Imbolc is a time of purification. The windows are opened in our houses and in our minds to let in fresh air and thought. It is a time for new beginnings and for emerging out of winter hibernation to begin the work of the coming year.

SPRING EQUINOX (DAWN)

The buds are unfurling, the Stag God is calling.

By Spring Equinox, we know that the seasons are really changing and that the life force is renewing. Birds are singing and nest building, the buds on the trees are opening their light green leaves, the colour which signifies spring.

To the ancient Germans, this was the festival of the Goddess Ostara, whose name comes from the same root as the female hormone oestrogen. Ostara's symbol is an egg, a symbol which appears today in some countries in the form of chocolate Easter eggs and in others as green-painted eggs, symbolic of spring fertility. There are many traditional customs associated with eggs which form part of Pagan celebrations today. In some countries eggs are hidden around the house and garden and children are sent out to search for them. In others, hard-boiled eggs are rolled downhill, with the fastest egg winning the race. Whatever the custom, it reminds us of the importance of the renewal of the life force.

This is also the time in the agricultural calendar when seeds are sown in the ploughed fields and when the hours of darkness are equal to the hours of light. All these elements may be woven into Spring celebrations. Often, a man will be chosen to represent the young Spring God and a woman the Spring Goddess. The God with his male companions will encounter the Goddess with her maidens. Sometimes one flees from the other, for 'otherness' is strange and threatening. We must become accustomed to it before we can accept it. There is courtship, advance and withdrawal, perhaps an exchange of gifts, until finally the two essential aspects of the life force come together and seeds may then be symbolically sown to indicate the beginning of the cycle of fertility. Often each member of a group sows seeds in pots of earth which are then carefully nurtured and the seedlings transplanted when they are strong. In this way the message of nurturing is conveyed to each one of us.

Solitary Pagans may tend their gardens and contemplate with the sowing of seeds for the coming season the power and endurance of the life force. We may try with our concrete to cover the Earth and shut Nature out, but always Nature is seeking to break through and remind us of her presence.

Imbolc is often a time to plan new projects. The Spring Equinox is a time to begin them. In Nature, birds have built their nests and now lay eggs. Astrologically, at Spring Equinox

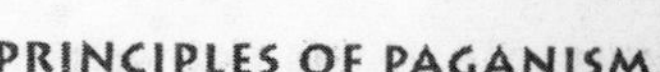

the Sun is considered to be in the sign of Aries. This is a sign of energy and activity. The plans and ideas we have formulated at Imbolc under the airy sign of Aquarius can now be given energy and life.

BELTANE (MID-MORNING)

The May Queen is crowned, and calleth her bridegroom.

At Beltane, the evidence of new life is everywhere. The trees are hung with sweet-smelling blossom. Birds are hatching their eggs. The trees are filled with birdsong. Dandelions and buttercups appear. Traditional May Day rites from the European traditions are strongly associated with fertility. In pre-Puritan Britain, young men and maidens would go into the woods together on May Eve to gather May blossoms. 'And,' Puritans noted disapprovingly, 'many would emerge no longer maids.' Rural life was much earthier than life today. Often the bedding would proceed the wedding, not only because young men and women are moved by the same impulses as today, but because in farming communities a man with fertile seed and a fertile wife who could bear children were essential. The work needed many hands and the more children, the more there were to work. Marriage often followed evidence of pregnancy.

Traditional May celebrations involved crowning a May Queen, a young woman of child-bearing age, who would process the village as a symbol of the young Goddess. In

Catholic countries there are sometimes similar processions today, but the young woman is under the guise of the Virgin Mary.

Another May Day tradition is May-pole dancing. Whereas the May Queen symbolizes the Goddess, it is the May-pole which symbolizes the God. The ribbons which are woven about the pole by the dancers celebrate the fertility of the God. May-pole dancing involves two circles of dancers. One circle dances sunwise (clockwise in the Northern Hemisphere and anti-clockwise in the South), which is often known by the Celtic name of deosil. The other circle dances anti-clockwise or widdershins (against the Sun). In Western Paganism the sunwise direction is associated with life and the widdershins direction with death. The May-pole dance interweaves the forces of life and death, creation and destruction, recognizing that death is the inevitable outcome of life and after death life is renewed. The God is the phallic creator God, but also the Lord of the Dead.

MIDSUMMER (NOON)

The God is his power must be king of the land.

At Midsummer the crops are growing, flowers blooming and young have been born to the herds in the fields, but nothing can endure and blossom forever. The message of the cosmos is change. The days have lengthened, but soon the shadows will stretch once more.

In Scandinavian countries, with their later seasonal cycle and truncated summer, Midsummer is a more important festival than May Day. In modern Sweden and also in Norway, Midsummer is treated as a holiday and fires are lit through Midsummer night to symbolize the power of the Sun. In the far North, the Sun is a most welcome visitor and the contrast between dark and light is great when in summer day may be 20 hours or longer, depending on how far North one is, and in winter night may be interminable.

Midsummer rites in Paganism are often dedicated to the Solar Hero. There have been many of these in myth and history, and in the boundary between the two. King Arthur was such a solar hero king. He fought for the powers of light and right against the forces of destruction and darkness, but he was a warrior in the service of his people rather than a fighter for fighting's sake. His sword was raised in the service of the feminine. There were three major women in his life, symbolic of the Triple Goddess – his dark half-sister Morgan, the fairy woman, whose names means 'the Woman of the Sea', and who, like the sisters of the ancient Pharaohs, was both his sister and the mother of his child; Gwenhwyfar or, in its French form, Guinevere, the golden-haired, his barren wife; and the mysterious Lady of the Lake, who entrusted to him the sword of justice, Excalibur, and took it back to the Otherworld beneath the waters when it was time for him to cross to the Otherworld in death.

The relationship between masculine and feminine is interwoven in the symbolism of Midsummer. The Sun King is at the height of his powers in the Northern Hemisphere when the sun is in the astrological sign of Cancer, ruled by the Moon and most feminine sign of the Zodiac. The true Solar Hero is therefore one who knows and honours the feminine within himself and within others.

A Celtic God who can be invoked at Midsummer is the Irish God Lugh, a God of Light. In Irish myth, like many solar heroes, Lugh slays the old king whose reign has become negative. In this case, the old king is Balor, Lugh's grandfather. Balor has shut himself away on an island and imprisoned his daughter Eithne because of a prophecy that his grandson will slay him. Eithne manages to bear sons, one of whom is Lugh. Balor casts them to the sea, but Lugh survives and returns in adulthood to slay him.

A battle between the God of the old year and the God of the new may form part of Pagan celebrations. The force of life is ever at war with the force of destruction and death. At the Midsummer battle, the young God slays the older God, but often in myths and legends the Solar Hero is wounded and gradually begins to lose his strength. This symbolizes that the days begin to shrink even though summer is still at full height.

Another theme which may be celebrated in Pagan rites is the marriage of the Sun God to the land. The land in Pagan myth is usually symbolized by a Goddess of Sovereignty. He who wins the Goddess has control over the land. The relationship between Goddesses of the Land and the holder of worldly power – the king – is an important theme in Celtic mythology. The Irish texts suggest that a king might be married to his tribal Goddess. This would take place as a Sacred Marriage with a priestess or even with the Goddess' symbolic animal. This relates to ancient ideas of family inheritance which were originally matrilinear – through the mother's descendants. Land would be passed down the female line and in order to become king, a warrior would marry a royal princess. This may have been the original reason why the Egyptian Pharaohs married their sisters. The Goddess Maeve of Connaught was said to have married nine kings of Ireland.

The Goddess is weeping, her sickle is stained.

Lughnasadh, the Games of Lugh, is the Irish name given to the festival of 1 August. It is also known by its Saxon name of *Lammas*, Loaf Mass. The loaf is the first loaf baked from the newly-gathered corn, for Lammas celebrates the corn harvest.

Once the corn was safely gathered, there would be time for general rejoicing. Yet death is present in many ways at Lammas. From Midsummer onwards the rays of the Sun have dried out the green stalks and ears of corn and wheat and what is gathered creates sweet grain to be ground into flour for bread and strong stalks of straw for animal feed and bedding (and at one time human bedding) for the winter; but what is gathered is essentially dead. The food of life comes from a plant baked dry by the Sun, which now begins to fade in strength.

The fields of ripened corn are also home to foxes, rabbits and other small creatures of the field. As the reapers cut their circular swathe from the outer edge of the fields to the inner, the animals are trapped at the centre. Around the edge, humans with cudgels wait for them to break their cover and attempt to flee. Usually they fail and there is meat for the pot, but also blood upon the corn; in the midst of Summer Sun and the grain of life is the blood of death. In fields of the past this reminder was present throughout the growing season. Untainted by chemical sprays, red poppies bloomed amongst the green and then golden corn. This reminder is important in Paganism, for Paganism does not romanticize Nature. The cycle of the seasonal festivals is a wheel, ever turning and moving onwards. If we understand this in our own lives, then we adapt and change. We take each day as a gift which is all the more precious because it is transient and we learn to extract hope, peace and joy from a draught which is inevitably mixed with bitterness.

Midsummer is the festival most associated with kingship. Lammas is associated with the death of the king. In Celtic lore, as with many tribal peoples, the king had to be in perfect health and sound of limb. His marriage with the land meant that the power of life was vested in him. If his strength failed and his powers waned then the land would become barren and the people would die. The Lammas festival is therefore often associated with the ritual slaying of the king. His blood is spilled on the reaped fields, his power and life force are thus returned to the land to renew it for the coming year. The king voluntarily sacrifices himself at the Goddess' hand to renew the land.

The message that life was transient came to our ancestors in other ways. Summer was the period of war. No one could sustain a winter campaign for long in days before waterproof clothing and rust-free steel. For our more warlike ancestors such as the Celts and Norse, the beginning of summer through to the corn harvest was a time for sea raids and cattle raids, a time to seek honour, glory, renown and plunder. Traditionally, hostilities were suspended at harvest time. Everyone was needed to gather the grain.

Lammas is also a Goddess festival and a time for celebrating the bounty of the Goddess of the Harvest. Once the harvest was gathered, people could cease work for a few days and enjoy a well-earned rest. Lugh's Games were celebrated with fairs, contests and revels. Cattle markets would be held, goods traded. In some areas, August fairs were hiring fairs. Farm workers and servants would contract with a master or mistress for a year and a day – that is, from 1 August to 1 August again – and then were free to seek a new master or mistress if they wished.

Another use of the harvest was in the making of ale. In English traditional folk-song this is celebrated by the song 'John Barleycorn', which tells of the sowing, ripening and harvesting of the barley, which is then transformed into 'home-brewed ale'. The message here is that found throughout the seasonal cycle and is a message for us all: the message of life, death and renewal.

The Goddess at Lammas is the bountiful Mother, but she is also the Crone, wielder of the sickle. Lammas is therefore a time of feminine transition. Its themes are about letting go and moving onwards in our life's journey. One of the lessons of middle life is that we too must at some point let go of our worldly success. Often in these days of enforced change this comes about through redundancy. It can also come about by our children growing up and leaving home. At this stage of our life we must re-examine our lives and values and decide whether outward, worldly orientation is still sufficient for our happiness. Often we will decide it is not and that it is time to make or renew our spiritual quest. Sometimes this can take us into new spiritual pathways. We may remain with our current path but re-examine our role in it, perhaps ceasing to take such an active part in outer organizing in order to make a spiritual retreat to renew the wellsprings of inspiration with us. We may also do this with our chosen profession, perhaps returning to further study to re-evaluate and update our approach. These themes begin at Lammas and continue at Autumn or Fall Equinox.

The roses are dead and the birds have gone
and the rain has washed away the Sun.

In most countries, academic terms or semesters begin around late August or September. In earlier, more agricultural-based societies this was a practical time for study once children were no longer needed to help out with the harvest. The corn harvest in most Northern Hemisphere countries is over in August, but other harvests continue into September. My mother, who is 79, remembers her class being taken into the fields in early September to help out with the potato harvest. In later September, it is time for the apple harvest.

The Autumn or Fall Equinox, like Lammas, is often celebrated as a harvest festival, this time for the remainder of the crops. In earlier societies this was a crucial time of reckoning: was there enough food to go round for the winter? Were all the storehouses full or would there be famine? At the Equinox the approach of the cold of winter is noticeable and our orientation changes from outwards and long sunny days outside to inside, inwards and the long dark nights.

Related to autumn are myths which explain the onset of winter and the disappearance of seasonal greenery. One of the best known of these is the myth of the Greek Goddess Demeter and her daughter Kore, who is also known as Persephone. Kore is stolen away by Hades, Lord of the Underworld, who wants her for his bride. Demeter is distraught and goes in search of her daughter. She blasts the land in her wrath and Nature begins to die. Eventually she discovers Hades' wrong-doing and has him summoned to Mount Olympus, the home of the Gods, for judgement. The judgement of the Gods is that Kore's time must be divided between her mother's realm of Earth and her husband's realm of the Underworld. For two thirds of the year, she will roam the Earth and Nature will grow. For the remainder, she will be beneath the Earth and this will be winter. This period corresponds roughly to the period between the Equinox and Imbolc when the Virgin Goddess reappears once more to renew the land. Pagan celebrations may take the form of a mystery play to enact the story of Demeter and Persephone. Smaller children may enjoy playing the parts of the trees, rivers, Sun and other natural phenomena which Demeter questions in her search for her daughter. Other celebrations take the form of harvest festivals and a special feast to celebrate the bounty of the land.

Another theme inherent in the Equinox is the equality between the hours of darkness and the hours of light, but here it is darkness which is in the ascendant. A good time for celebrations is therefore sunset, for we are entering the darker time of the year.

Autumn is also associated with turning inwards in another sense. The Equinox tides and winds may bring storm and shipwreck and are considered in Paganism to be a time of transition. This is apparent in the world of Nature. Leaves fall from the trees, birds migrate, the signs of life disappear one by one. The Mystery Initiations of Eleusis in Greece took place at this time and for those of us on a spiritual path it can be a good time to turn inwards and renew our own dedication to our chosen path. Some Pagan groups practise mystery initiation rites which are designed to show through symbol and enactment important messages about the meaning of life and death.

There are many Pagan myths and legends which are based around the theme of descending into the Underworld to attain spiritual knowledge. The Sumerian and Babylonian myths of the descent of the Goddess to understand the mystery of death are initiatory rites of this kind. A similar story of the Goddess' descent is found in the Northern Tradition where Freya, the Goddess of Fertility, descends into the Underworld to gain the necklace *Brisingamen*, Bright Fire. In Pagan myth a necklace is often symbolic of the circle of life, death and rebirth. There are also Pagan myths of male descent into the Underworld to overcome death. The descent of the Greek musician Orpheus to rescue his wife Euridyce is one such myth. Another myth which hints at male initiation by the Goddess is that told in the Norse poem *Hyndluljóth* in which the Goddess Freya takes her lover Ottar down into the Underworld to learn his ancestry.

In the Northern Tradition, there is also a myth of reversal which is an initiatory experience. This is the ordeal of Odin strung upside-down on the World Tree to gain the secret of the runes.

All these initiatory myths can be the basis for Equinox celebrations for adult Pagans.

SAMHAIN/HALLOWE'EN

In the dark of the night, the ancestors walk.

Samhain is celebrated by many Pagans as the Celtic New Year, though it is by no means certain that this was the beginning of New Year in all Celtic areas. Other Pagans take Imbolc, the return of the Goddess to the land, as the beginning of the year.

Most people will be more familiar with Samhain than with some of the other Pagan festivals because of customs associated with Hallowe'en and, in England, Bonfire Night. At Samhain we know that we are entering winter and indeed its Celtic name meant Summer's End. Winter brought snow and frost and meant that only a few animals would have enough grass to graze and fodder for their indoor feeding. Many animals had to be slaughtered and their meat salted for the winter. Samhain was therefore associated with death in a very real way. It also had death associations for other reasons. With the onset of cold, the death rate would go up, something which is still true today. Samhain was therefore treated as a festival of the dead, a time for remembering those who had gone before, many of whom might have in any event died around this time of the year.

Our Celtic ancestors had great reverence for the head, which was considered the seat of inspiration and learning. Heads of worthy opponents would be cut off and taken back to display in the communal hall. This may seem barbaric to Pagans today, but our ancestors' lives were harsher and rawer than our own and they did not share our physical squeamishness. Remnants of the veneration of the head are found at Samhain in the custom of hollowing out pumpkins, carving faces in them and placing candles inside these 'Jack O'Lanterns' to light the Samhain feast.

Other customs reflect the desire to commune at this time with the ancestors. Often an extra place would be set at the feast and food left out all night for dead relatives who might come and visit during Samhain night.

Samhain was a time when the veil between this world and the Otherworld was thin. Spirits of those who had died could return to visit their families and would aid with divination. The links between this season and death are apparent in those countries which stage Remembrance Day celebrations for the dead of the World Wars and other wars. Many people will be familiar with the red poppies which are sold to raise funds for former servicemen and women. The red poppy, the Lammas symbol of blood upon the corn, still reminds our secular society of death.

Many Samhain customs – such as apple bobbing – involve apples. The apple was considered a mysterious fruit which had something about it of the Otherworld. The Avalon of Arthurian myth was the Apple Isle. By cutting an apple horizontally across its middle we reveal that in the centre is a pentacle, the symbol of life. Apples are also associated with overcoming death in Northern European mythology, where eating the golden apples guarded by the Goddess Idun gave the Gods eternal youth.

One traditional custom is to peel an apple, keeping the peel in one continuous strand, and then to throw the skin over one's shoulder. The pattern in which it falls will show the first initial of the name of one's lover to come. There is a polarity here between the themes of Samhain and its opposite festival Beltane, a meeting of love and death.

Samhain is a time of coming to terms with death, something which many of us find very difficult. This may not be the death of the body, but of other things which we have lost during the year – relationships, jobs, material wealth. Samhain takes place during the astrological sign of Scorpio, which is ruled by the element of Water and especially the sea. Water transforms and changes. It washes away pain and sadness and Samhain is a good time to meditate on letting go of past hurts and wrongs. Often when people die we have unfinished business with them

– some things which we should have said and others which we would rather now not have said. One way of communing with our dead friends and family at this time is to write a letter which can then be sent to the Otherworld by being burned in the Samhain fire. On a practical level, it is a good time to tend the graves of our relatives if we have them.

YULE

In the deadness of winter, the spark of new life.
I have news for you:
the stag bells,
Winter snows,
Summer has gone,
wind high and cold.
Sun low, short its course,
sea running high.
Rust brown bracken, its shape lost,
the wild goose raises her accustomed cry.
Cold seizes the bird's wing;
season of ice:
this is my news.

NINTH CENTURY IRISH POEM.

The Winter Solstice marks an important transition and one which was eagerly awaited by our ancestors. The Solstice is the nadir of the year, its lowest point in terms of daylight and energy, after which the year begins to turn. Many Christmas customs are adapted from Paganism – the bringing in of a special Yule log, feasting, games and celebration. Bringing an evergreen tree into the house and decorating it is also a Pagan custom. Amongst the bare and skeletal deciduous trees, the evergreen stands as a sign of hope that spring will one day return to the land; so too the bright red berried holly. All these were brought into the house to decorate it for the Yule feast.

The word 'Yule' comes from the Germanic languages and was to our Germanic ancestors what the feast of Samhain was to the Celts. It was a time for gathering in the communal hall, of eating and drinking; a time to listen to the skalds weave stories of the summer exploits of heroes to inspire them and others to emulate them in the coming year; a time to satirize those who had performed mean and unworthy actions and so to discourage others from emulating these; a time to sing of adventure and of love. Our Germanic ancestors spent 12 days celebrating Yule, hence the carol 'The Twelve Days of Christmas'.

Pagans celebrate and give gifts at Yule, a custom which Pagan children are keen to encourage because they can probably convince long-suffering parents that 'like everybody else' they ought to get Christmas presents as well.

Many Pagans celebrate the birth of the Sun Child, the Child of Promise, who will mature and become the young God of Spring. This time of year was celebrated as the birth of the Sun Child long before Christianity, which later adopted it as a matter of convenience for the birth date of its own God. The emphasis in Pagan Yule celebrations, however, is not only on the Sun Child but also on his Mother. Celebrations will honour the Great Mother Goddess who brings new life and hope to the land.

Pagans celebrate the seasonal cycle. How else do they honour their Gods?

SACRED TIME, SACRED PLACE, SACRED SPACE

The purpose of spiritual practice is to draw nearer the Gods, the Divine source of all things. Two ways of doing this are through developing a sense of Sacred Time and Sacred Place.

SACRED TIME

Celebrating the seasonal cycle is one way of creating Sacred Time. We can also create Sacred Time on a daily, weekly or monthly basis by setting aside time which is not devoted to maintaining our physical bodies, earning our living, caring for families, developing our intellects through study or our physical prowess through sport. It is setting aside time to honour the Divine force which gives life to the universe.

When people think of someone as 'religious', they often mean that he or she visits a place of communal worship – a church, synagogue, mosque or temple. Communal worship is not essential in Paganism. If the Divine is everywhere, including within ourselves, we do not have to go out to meet it; nor do we need to share our religious expression with others. Pagans may choose to observe Sacred Time with others or they may not. The choice is an individual one.

We may set aside Sacred Time in many ways. In most spiritual systems, there is some form of observance at the beginning and end of each day and sometimes at special times throughout the day as well. Observance is a matter of individual choice in Paganism. Some Pagans meditate or pray at the beginning and/or end of each day. This may be done indoors. Others may have a place in their garden they visit each day to remind themselves of who and what they are and of their place in the universe.

Some Pagans pray. Polytheistic Pagans see different Gods as personages dwelling in another realm. Their approach to their Deities is not so different from how a monotheist might see his or her God, except that a Pagan might pray to a number of Deities.

Other Pagans see their Deities not as separate beings but as different expressions of the Divine Unity. Pantheistic Pagans who see the Divine in All tend to speak of meditating on or communing with the Divine rather than praying. Meditation may involve contemplating a particular God or Goddess image in order to come to an understanding of what this aspect of the Divine means in our own lives. Meditation can, however, be much more abstract and involve emptying the mind of thought, stilling the busy byways of consciousness and entering a state of interior stillness in which the boundaries of self and other are dissolved.

Honouring the day by simple words of welcome is a powerful way of linking ourselves with the greater universe and reminding ourselves that we are not alone in it. It is part of us and we of it. This welcome may be a simple phrase:

Hail to thee, O Sun, in thy rising,
thou comest forth in beauty, O my Lady of Light.

or our greeting may be wordless. Observance of Sacred Time may be as simple as someone coming home from the end of a day's work, washing, lighting a candle on his or her altar, entering for a few moments into the interior stillness of meditation, then extinguishing the light and making the children's supper. What those few moments will have given us, brief though they may be, is a reminder that despite the frenzy of the world around us, there is within us a place of peace and harmony which is a reflection of the deeper peace and harmony of the Divine. Another way to help us focus our lives is to keep a personal journal in which we reflect upon our lives at the end of each day.

Many people have irregular and hectic lives. This makes daily spiritual practice difficult. Another approach is to set aside blocks of time for vigils, retreats or vision quests. Vigils, long periods spent in meditation at a selected spot, can be an important way of overcoming our habits of thought and opening ourselves to new inspiration. Celtic bards would spend nights at ancient burial mounds in order to commune with the spirit of the past and to receive new inspiration for their artistic expression.

Vision quests, which involve fasting and spending time outside in a Sacred Place, are common in many Pagan cultures. These help us separate ourselves for a time from our everyday concerns to focus on what is really important – our inner spirit which is eternal and enduring. Vision quests are largely solitary, but there are activities which can be carried out with others. In the Native American tradition, sweat lodges are important ceremonies of purification which bind communities together in shared spiritual experience. In Northern Europe, similar practices were carried out by peoples whose ancestry was not so distantly removed, in the form of the sauna. Saunas, like sweat lodges, are not only a practical method of cleansing the body where bathing water is not available. They are also spiritual occasions and social ritual.

Retreats in Pagan, non-denominational or ecumenical settings can also help renew the wellsprings of our spirituality. Meeting with others of like mind but from different spiritual paths can be a source of great joy. They help us see that although our religions may be superficially different we are all seeking in our own ways to know the Divine.

SACRED PLACE

To Pagans, all the Earth is sacred, but certain places have always been seen as holy places, where the veil between this world and the Otherworld is thin. Our ancestors thought particular spots had a *genius loci*, a spirit of the place. This can be thought of either as a particular atmosphere which the place invokes, or as a personality or entity. The landscape of Europe contains holy wells, sacred mountains, mysterious standing stones and earth barrows, many of whose purposes we can only guess. Similar sacred sites, power points, places of pilgrimage and burial grounds are found across the landscape of North America, Australia and other countries.

Sometimes these sacred sites are natural formations. Places where two elements meet are often considered particularly sacred – high mountains where earth meets air, the place between sea and shore, springs which emerge from deep beneath the earth, waterfalls which cascade through the air, caves which go deep into the earth. Other places evoke a sense of wildness – woodlands where few humans go, moorlands swept by the power of wind, and the great sea.

Trees and groves were particularly sacred to our ancestors and one of the first acts of Christian missionaries was to chop down the sacred groves of those they were seeking to convert

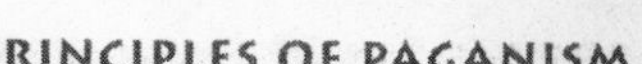

from their Pagan Deities. Trees have always been evocative to those who see the Divine as manifest in Nature. Trees outlive human beings. Indeed, some trees, such as the great sequoia trees of California, are older than Christianity. Trees represent continuity, endurance and wisdom. Deciduous trees are living images of the seasonal cycle of death, rest, reawakening and renewal and are therefore symbols of hope. They are also important to us in a very practical way. They are the lungs of our planet and maintain the oxygen in our atmosphere. While our ancestors may not have understood all the ins and outs of the biological cycle, on an intuitive level they understood much better than we trees' importance.

There are many ways in which we can gain a sense of Sacred Place. We can choose a Sacred Place and visit it each festival to see how it changes with the seasons. Alternatively, we can choose eight different places, one for each festival.

Your Sacred Place might be an ancient site which has been used by Pagans long ago. It might be a place which is evocative and meaningful for you. Meditate there, picnic, dance or perform a simple ritual. Different festivals have associations with different times of day and exploring sacred sites at different hours can be very rewarding. The site which seems mundane by day may be powerful and mysterious at night when the tourists have gone home. The site which seems warm and friendly by day may be a strange place indeed at dawn.

Worshipping at ancient sites is something which attracts many Pagans, but care and sensitivity is needed. In North America and Australia, Europeans are recent immigrants. The sacred sites of the land are those of other peoples and we must respect their right to restrict access to them if they wish. In Europe, the Neolithic spirits of a burial mound might not appreciate our holding a full-scale Pagan celebration there. Our midnight drumming, while delightfully evocative to us, might seem no more than a rowdy party. On the other hand, if we visit a site over a period of time, if we commemorate the spirits of those who made it in time-honoured fashion by making offerings of food and beer, then our presence may be very welcome even if our Paganism bears only a passing resemblance to their own.

We must also respect sites on a practical level. If too many people use ancient sites, we will damage them. If we use woodland for our rites, we should be careful that we do not damage trees. (I have seen urban Pagans building a ritual fire next to the trunk of an ancient oak.) We must also take home with us our urban litter.

GET TO KNOW YOUR LOCAL ENVIRONMENT

Connecting with the Divine in Nature is not only a spiritual exercise. Most of us know little about our locality or the other life forms which inhabit it. How many of us can recognize its trees, birds, wild animals, flowers and herbs? There is a language which tells us about natural cycles, but we have forgotten it. If we learn to recognize the birds in our fields, woods, parks and gardens, we will get to know their seasonal migrations. We will learn to recognize by the birds' early departure if winter is to be harsh. If we learn to look at clouds and to register the direction of the wind, we will know when rain is coming, when we are likely to get a storm. This is no longer essential knowledge as it was when humans were dependent on farming, fishing and hunting for their livelihood, but when we are ignorant we walk about in a kind of blindness. A return to Paganism is a return to seeing.

It is not only visiting Sacred Places which is important, but also getting there. Walking to sacred sites or pilgrimages is an important part of all religious traditions. To walk along an ancient path to a sacred site is to walk a way that generations and generations have walked before with a spiritual purpose in mind. These energies will be imprinted upon the landscape and, in tuning into these patterns, we tune into the sense of reverence of those who have gone before.

Walking the land is one way of 'reconnecting'. Another is living on it or from it. Many Pagan rituals and events take place outside and in summer in active Pagan countries there are camps which enable us to live close to Nature for a while. Often there are opportunities to learn ancient crafts such as making fire with wood or flint, herbalism, weaving and other skills which, though once accessible, have now become a mysterious lost knowledge. These things are important because without them we are like children in Nature. We are unable to use what is around us and we can no longer fend for ourselves. This does not mean that Pagans wish to return to a full-time life of self-sufficiency (though some do), but such skills are empowering. We may not all want to live off the land, but growing some of our own food – even if it is only tomatoes or herbs in a window box – enables us to reconnect with the cycles of growth in Nature.

There are other ways of learning to know our environment, such as learning to dowse. Within the pattern of the land are earth energies, points of power and transmutation. Some of these lie along what are known as ley lines. At one time each village had its dowser who would locate underground water for sinking a well. The dowser would also know good sites to build a house, places where the energy was not liable to cause sickness. In China this art, known as Feng Shui, was highly developed and is still practised by the Chinese today.

It is not only the daylight world we need to know, but also the world of night. Above our heads in the night sky is a universe of myriad beauty, filled with planets, stars, shooting stars – all signs that life exists beyond our world. The night sky opens us to worlds of wonder even with the naked eye. With a small telescope we can see a universe of incredible beauty.

It was by turning their minds, hearts and spirits to these outer things that our ancestors learned to love and cherish the universe in which they had been born. If we close our eyes to the beauty of the night, we lose a window into a wider world which shows us that humanity's place in it is small. Strangely enough, this is not threatening, but humbling and joyful. When we are beset by our own problems and concerns, looking outwards and seeing the reality of their smallness allows us to stand back; to see things in perspective; to understand that all things pass and so too will anxiety, pain and fear. By looking outward, we rekindle our hope.

REMEMBERING TIME – KNOWING PLACE – LOCAL CUSTOMS

Within the traditional calendar of all countries are customs and ceremonies of Pagan origin. Some of these have fallen into disuse except in rural areas, but one way of renewing our Paganism is to revive traditional customs. These do not have to be reserved exclusively for Pagans. There are many customs which the whole community can enjoy and which make valuable links between people of different beliefs, both spiritual and secular. If you look in books of local folklore, you will find customs such as May celebrations, well-dressing, times when sacred hills and sites would be visited. Schools and other community organizations can often be persuaded to help revive these.

In England, the custom of beating the bounds is undergoing a revival. This is carried out in May on what is known in the Christian calendar as Rogation Sunday. Beating the bounds is a relic of spring fertility rites and combines giving magical encouragement to the crops with affirming shared land rights.

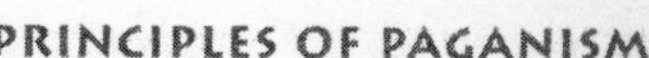

Village families meet and walk the village boundaries. The children carry willow wands which are used to hit boundary stones and other prominent features of the bounds. This shows each succeeding generation the village boundaries and also prevents landowners from infringing on common land. Fences put across common land are torn down and public footpaths which have been blocked off are reopened. Hiking and rambling clubs are often interested in this idea.

These are all useful ways for people to be introduced to Pagan ideas, reminding us of our relationship to our environment and, equally importantly, binding communities together in a highly mobile age when we are not all closely related, working for a common employer, long-standing residents of our localities or sharing a common religion. Many who see themselves as being of other faiths or of no faith at all find meaning in reconnecting themselves with the place they live and in shared communal activity.

CREATIVE PAGANISM

Ancient theatre derived from religious ceremonies and mystery plays designed to help us understand our relationships to the Gods and to the wider universe. In Eastern societies, festivals with dragons, performers dressed as mythological figures, ceremonial wagons bearing images of the Gods and plays which illustrate mythological and religious themes are all very familiar. In the Western world, these are also familiar in Mediterranean Catholic countries whose religion was never sanitized by the Protestant Reformation.

Today, there has been a great revival through performance art of ritual theatre and it is now part of the syllabus in many drama schools. Ritual theatre has also become important in the Pagan community, as Pagans have started to meet in large outdoor gatherings. Wordy rites are of little use in a field full of

thousands of people, so there has been a return to ritual processions and the use of evocative symbols such as giants, wicker men, fire mazes, dance, drumming, music and chanting as a way of unifying Pagans in celebration and honouring the Gods. These methods of celebrating Sacred Time have also become more important as the number of Pagan families has grown. Children enjoy this type of religious celebration and can have a valued role rather than being bored bystanders.

Other ways of representing archetypal themes are through games. Tugs of war between summer and winter express in living symbol the dynamic of growth and decay which we celebrate in our seasonal cycle. Egg hunts for children illustrate the return of fertility to the land. Folk dances evoke many of the themes of life and death. Many of these are present in Morris dancing, particularly in what is known as Bedlam or Black Morris, where the participants black their faces and are dressed in the colourful rags of mummers rather than the more familiar white trousers and white shirts. Creative participation is a way of taking the messages of Paganism back to where they belong – to the people – so that all can access them at the level they wish.

The arts are involved in Paganism in other ways. Many forms of Paganism focus on developing creativity as a way of celebrating our spirituality and of increasing and enhancing it. Creating poetry, plays, ritual prose, songs, chants, music and dance to honour the Gods helps us engage in our celebrations, so that they are not performances by others, but something to which we contribute our energy and power. These need not be complex. Circle dance is a very simple way of entering into a state of tranquillity and harmony which becomes a living, moving meditation. Many Westerners are unattracted by the more static forms of meditation but rhythmical movement and sound are other ways in which we can still the over-busy

conscious mind, so that it allows us the space within to commune with and enter into oneness with the Divine.

RITES IN PAGAN LIFE

All the more organized forms of Paganism – the Northern Tradition, Druidry and Wicca – involve group ritual. Ritual is also a feature of non-aligned Pagan groups. Four major types of ritual are found in Paganism:

Observances of Sacred Time: the celebrations of the seasonal cycle and in some traditions Full and possibly New Moon celebrations;

Rites of passage to mark transitions in the life cycle – birth, maturity, marriage, giving birth, ageing and death;

Initiation rituals which take adult initiates into closer understanding of the Divine Mysteries;

Rituals for specific intentions – healing rituals, eco-magic rituals to enlist the aid of the Gods in protecting the environment.

SACRED SPACE

Pagans are creative and spontaneous in the way they honour their Gods and rites vary between the traditions. However, there are some typical patterns.

Pagan rites may take place anywhere. They are not confined to a particular building designated as a church. Often, Pagans prefer not to celebrate their rites indoors, but instead to find a quiet place outside beneath the open sky and with their feet upon the earth. Often Pagan ritual takes place in woods and fields. Some Pagans will create a space in their gardens for their rites. Perhaps they will plant a circle of trees or mark the space with a circle of stones. Venerating the Divine outside in the world of Nature is important because Nature is the mirror of the Divine. In the pattern of the seasons, we see the ever-renewing and ever-changing life force and in attuning ourselves to the seasonal cycle around us, we can come to an understanding of the greater cosmos.

Outdoor ritual is not always practical and rites may take place in Pagans' own homes. A special room may be set aside or there may be a small shrine in the corner of bedroom or living-room. Some may have a statue of a Goddess or God on their altar. These may be beautiful and humanoid images such as those of ancient Greece and Rome, but they may be much simpler – a rounded rock which is suggestive of a pregnant woman, a piece of bark which appears to have eyes as though the Green Man himself were looking out through them. Some Pagans keep symbols of the Four Elements on their altars – a candle for Fire, incense for Air, a bowl of water for Water and rock, crystal or a bowl of earth for Earth. Other objects of natural beauty may be added to remind us of the natural world around us – flowers, a plant, a feather, a shell. Pagans do not worship these objects, or indeed statues of the Gods. Their role is to remind us of the Divinity which lies beyond them.

CREATING SACRED SPACE

Group ritual often takes place in a circle or square with a central altar or fire. If you think about the layout of Christian churches, you will realize that this is different from the Sacred Space which has been used in the West over the past millennium or so. Churches were built as rectangles with God at one end and human beings at the other. In medieval Churches and in Orthodox Christianity, there is even a screen about a third of the way down the church which is closed at the most sacred

part of the celebration. Only the ordained male priest is worthy enough to experience the mystery. In Pagan rites, the Divine force is seen as being at the centre. This is not only the centre of the group of worshippers but also the centre of ourselves, for Pagans believe that each of us is at our core Divine. Each of us is also part of the priesthood – if that is our wish. We can create our own rites and forms of worship and have no need of priestly hierarchy to authorize and sanction them.

Circular rites are common in Goddess groups and in WiseCraft, where magic may be part of the rites. The circle is thought of as a container for magical energy which is raised within the circle and which must be focused and contained before it is 'sent' to do its work. But not all Pagan rites are carried out in circular space. Rites for the veneration of Deities do not necessarily need this type of space, though many use it.

Entry to Sacred Space may be marked in a number of ways. Some traditions wear special dress or robes. Others remove their shoes or if outside wear special sandals. Watches are usually removed, for Sacred Space is considered to be outside the laws of human measured time and time should not be a preoccupation of those within it.

Often the boundaries of Sacred Space are marked out to signify that the space has been set apart. They may be physical if a circle of stones has been made or if the rite takes place in a room specially set aside for worship, but often the boundaries will be marked by drawing a circle around the space with a staff or ritual knife or sword, either symbolically in the air or physically on the ground.

There may be a ceremonial procession of the Four Elements – sprinkling the boundaries with water to which salt (considered a symbol of the element of Earth) has been added, censing them and bearing light or fire around them. Air, Fire, Water and Earth are thought of as energy in different forms, from the least to the most solid. These four symbols represent the whole of material creation. In Nature the elements are seen as the air we breathe, the Sun which warms us, the waters of which our bodies are mainly comprised and the earth which produces the bounty which nourishes us. These are the forces necessary for life and are therefore honoured.

Most Western Paganism, like Native American and other indigenous traditions, honours the sacred directions of East, South, West and North. This is a symbolic way of honouring the land around us. The quarters are often thought of as Gateways which allow communion with different aspects of the spiritual realm. In Western Paganism, the Four Directions are associated with the Four Elements: Air in the East, Fire in the South, Water in the West, Earth in the North. By addressing the Four Directions, we are symbolically addressing the whole of existence. The ceremonial salutation may take place by taking a symbol of the element to the appropriate quarter and invoking the presence of the Elemental powers to protect the Sacred Space.

The circle guarded by the Four Quarters is symbolized by the circle-cross and appears in the symbolism of many Pagan peoples. This is what Black Elk, a Holy Man of the Oglala Lakota, said about circles and the Four Quarters:

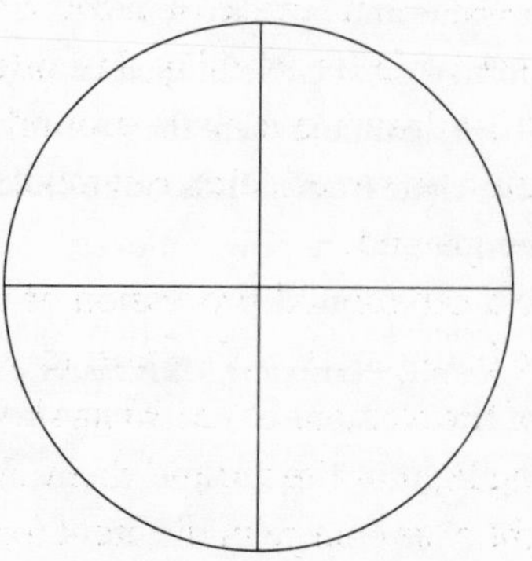

You will have noticed
that everything an Indian does is in a circle,
and that is because the Power of the World always works in circles,
and everything tries to be round.
In the old days, when we were a strong and happy people,
all our power came to us from the sacred hoop of the nation,
and so long as the hoop was unbroken, the people flourished.
The flowering tree was the living centre of the hoop,
and the circle of the four quarters nourished it.
The East gave peace and light,
the South gave warmth,
the West gave rain,
and the North with its cold and mighty wind
gave strength and endurance.
This knowledge came to us from the outer world with our religion.
Everything the Power of the World does is done in a circle.
The sky is round, and I have heard,
that the Earth is round like a ball,
and so are all the stars.
The wind, in its greatest power, whirls.
Birds make their nest in circles,
for theirs is the same religion as ours.
The Sun comes forth and goes down again in a circle.
The Moon does the same and both are round.
Even the seasons form a great circle in their changing,
and always come back again to where they were.
The life of a man is a circle from childhood to childhood,
and so it is in everything where power moves.

Black Elk Speaks: Being the Life Story of a Holy Man of the Oglala Sioux,
John G. Neihardt, University of Nebraska Press,
Lincoln and London, 1979.

Once Sacred Space has been created, the Gods are addressed in a form appropriate to the Tradition. Some Traditions practise invocation – an individual enters a state of trance and incarnates the Deity for the duration of the rite. The person may be pre-chosen or ecstatic dance may lead to the Deity manifesting through one or more of the dancers. In Western Paganism, incarnation of the Deity tends to be practised more by Pagans who see their Gods as different aspects of the Divine force and as communication links between humanity and the Divine. Polytheistic Pagans who see the Gods as separate beings may prefer to address them through prayer rather than through embodiment in an individual.

The invocation of the Gods may be followed by enactment of a seasonal myth, by rites of passage, or by specific prayers or magic to achieve particular ends, such as healing for individuals or for the land.

Not all Pagans practise magic and for many this holds no appeal. The very word is strange in our modern society. Magic as practised by Pagans involves uniting the minds of a group to a common purpose and visualizing that coming about by an act of focused will. The rationale of magic is too complex to explain here, but recent advances in science and our understanding of morphogenetic fields lend more rather than less credit to some of the magical ideas of so-called primitive peoples.

If we celebrate the festivals with others, mystery plays based on the seasonal themes are evocative ways of conveying their meaning. These are also useful because they can involve all the family, from the smallest upwards, in writing words, creating songs and dances, drumming and making music, making costumes, cooking appropriate food, decorating the altar and creating the ritual space. Pagan celebration is true celebration and although it may have moments of solemnity, the aim is always to create a balance of mirth and reverence, laughter and insight, understanding and mystery. It does not matter if babies cry and the dog decides to eat the ritual biscuits. These are all part of life's pattern and can be accommodated easily, providing we do not take ourselves too seriously.

Being *at ease* with oneself is one of the gifts of those who are truly spiritually enlightened. Those who have been recognized as people of true spiritual insight and to whom others have turned in past centuries for guidance have been renowned for their joy. This is understood more easily in the East, where we find sacred images such fat-bellied laughing Buddhas and of Ganesh the elephant-headed Hindu God with one tusk who enjoys a good joke. In the West, often religion has been obsessed with guilt, sin, asceticism and duty, rather than the joy of life. The Protestant work ethic was a useful ethos for a capitalist society wishing to increase its material wealth, but the pursuit of riches has not brought joy or harmony to the world.

Most Pagan rites will end with the sharing of wine, beer or mead and either token food in the form of bread or specially baked cakes, or a full-scale feast. Feasting is more likely to form part of seasonal celebrations and will involve traditional foods appropriate to the season. The feast is not considered a separate or lesser part of the celebration, but an equally important one. It is a way of enjoying the bounty of the Gods and of sharing it with others.

THE WHEEL OF THE YEAR AND THE WHEEL OF LIFE

On one hand, Pagan festivals are thanksgivings for the eternally-renewing cycle of Nature. The seasonal myths also mirror the human life cycle of conception, birth, maturation, decay and destruction. Rites of passage also mark these transitions.

Why do we celebrate the biological imperatives which rule our lives? Much of human life is a fight against reality. We seek

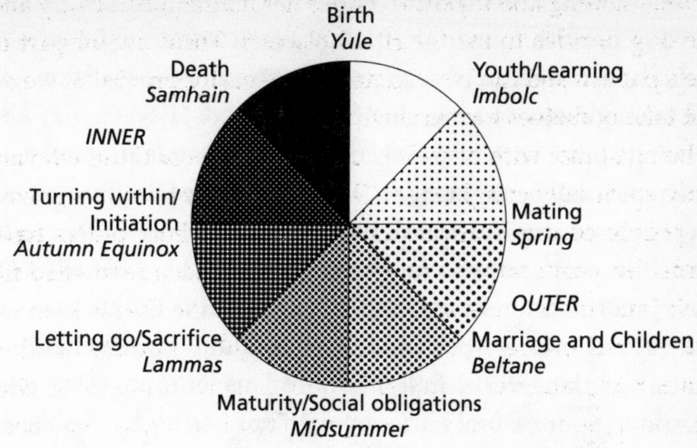

The Wheel of the Year and the Wheel of Life.

to deny ageing, illness, pain and death, when these are the inevitable lot of all of us, though maybe to a much lesser extent than we fear. Ageing and death are often unacceptable because we fear change. We fear to let go of the power, abilities and the world which we have known and to enter the unknown. One of the messages of Paganism is that life is change. We cannot stand still in this ever-evolving cosmos of ours. Time and change march on regardless. The answer lies in accepting change and in finding a way of rejoicing in it rather than fearing it.

The seasonal festivals of Paganism have a very important message: that the Wheel of the Year turns from darkness to light and back to darkness again; from ploughing, sowing, growth, fruition, reaping, harvest, sleeping, renewal to ploughing again. Our individual lives and destinies come and go, but the life force itself endures, remanifests and moves on.

Most of us wish to mark important life occasions – the birth of a child, marriage, death – through community celebration and the calling down of a blessing from the Gods. Pagans may also celebrate other rites which would be familiar to a tribal society, but which have not been so widely observed in the modern world. Some have devised rites of passage which mark the transition from adolescence to adulthood. These usually take place shortly after sexual maturation and it is not unusual, in the US Pagan press particularly, to find announcements celebrating a daughter's first menses. This is seen as part of reclaiming our natural harmony with our bodies and losing the sense of shame which Christianity has imposed on the body in recent centuries. At the other end of life, becoming an elder and an adviser rather than an organizer in the community is another important transition point. Initiation, in the sense of a personal experience of opening to the Divine, may also be celebrated. Initiation may occur at more than one stage of life and at differing levels. Some Pagan communities have three or more initiation ceremonies which mark transitions through spiritual change.

Pagans do not necessarily call upon a more experienced member of the community to perform their rites of passage. Many parents will arrange their own naming ceremonies for their children. Pagans who are marrying, or handfasting, as it is often called, may choose to conduct much of the rite themselves. Conducting our own funerals is somewhat tricky and here an experienced community member is likely to be called on. In Britain, the Pagan Hospice and Funeral Trust has been set up to help Pagans arrange their funerals.

In Paganism, rites of passage are seen as times of celebration and joy. This may seem strange in connection with funeral rites, but the emphasis in Pagan funerals is on honouring the person who has departed from us, but also on celebrating his or her life and achievements and celebrating his or her entry into the Otherworld.

Celebrating death may seem morbid to the modern mind. We tend to shut death out. Instead of dying in their homes, people are taken to sterile hospital environments where dying is tended by strangers and is not treated with reverence as one of the most important transitions of our lives – one it is important to do well and with family and friends about us.

In some religions, death holds fear because people may be condemned to eternal pain. This is not the belief of Paganism. Death is a transition which gives us time for rest, reflection and to see ourselves objectively. Where we have done wrong we will know sorrow, but death is also an initiatory experience whereby we gain the insight to restore what we have damaged.

In Paganism, death is treated as a friend with whom we can put down the burden of life and age and go forward into new life. Although our bodies decay, life endures. We live, die and will live again, though in another form. It is a belief of hope and optimism. However, dark our lives may seem, we know there will be release from pain and fear and liberation into a new life. After a time of rest, we are renewed once more to live and to live again. This is the message of the life force.

If Pagan's practices resonate with you, how can you find out more?

7

EXPLORING FURTHER

This book can offer only a brief glimpse of the richness of modern Paganism. If you wish to explore further, there are books which can help you understand Paganism more deeply. If you want to go beyond reading to a more active involvement, you are recommended to obtain magazines and join organizations which cover your area of interest.

Meeting other Pagans is not always easy. In some areas, there are open religious gatherings. You can find out about these through local esoteric book stores and Pagan magazines. The listings below cover magazines with a wide circulation. There are also regional magazines which will list local activities. You will find these listed in the national magazines. Magazines will list events, conferences, summer camps and groups which meet for teaching, discussion and/or worship. Attending a one-day conference or gathering can be a useful 'no commitment' way of having a look at Pagans and their ideas and deciding whether or not this is a compatible path for you.

If you are interested in a particular Pagan tradition, the national organizations can facilitate contacts with local groups. Where there is no local group, many organizations can provide home study training. Joining some Pagan traditions may involve a period of training and instruction and passing through a formal induction or initiation ceremony. Whether this is open to you may depend upon your age. Some Pagan paths believe that undertaking a particular religious path is more in the nature of answering a vocation, that is, responding to a call from the Gods. This is not something we are able to do until we reach adulthood.

When contacting any group which claims to represent a spiritual path, it is important to use your common sense. Perfectly sane people who have successful careers requiring sound judgements to be made in the outer world will suspend all rationality when approaching religious groups. Hundreds of people daily join cults which demand large joining fees, obedience to 'gurus' and 'masters', and take over their lives. Fortunately, Paganism has not generally been afflicted with such exploitative organizations, but this does not mean it could never occur. If you have doubts about a Pagan group that you approach, write to one of the larger European or US Pagan organizations for advice.

All Pagan organizations and magazines are run on donations and tight budgets. If you write, you cannot expect to receive a reply unless you send postage. In your own country, send a stamped addressed envelope and an extra stamp to cover administration costs. To overseas addresses, send two International Reply Coupons. These can be bought in large post offices and exchanged for stamps all over the world. Do not send cheques in your own currency to addresses overseas. The cost of cashing them is usually greater than the value of the cheque. Please write your address on any letter you send, in case letters and covering envelopes are separated. (As an ex-volunteer mail sorter for a Pagan organization, I know this happens frequently.)

The magazines and organizations listed are those which have

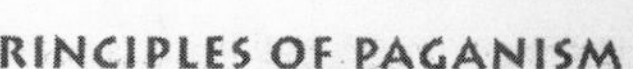

been running for some time and have relatively stable addresses. All have different orientations and the organizations can evolve and change with time. A listing does not necessarily imply recommendation. You must judge for yourself. If you run a Pagan group or organization which is not in touch with the major groups listed here, you may wish to contact them to foster networking and contacts.

PAGANISM OF THE PAST

BOOKS

The first book to attempt an overview of Paganism from ancient times to today is Prudence Jones and Nigel Pennick, *A History of Pagan Europe*, Routledge, London, 1995.

Ronald Hutton of Bristol University has written an interesting and scholarly account of early Paganism in Britain: *Pagan Religions of the Ancient British Isles*, Blackwell, Oxford, 1991. His conservative interpretations of the historical evidence might displease some, but are a useful reminder that reconstructing our Pagan past is a difficult task.

MODERN PAGANISM

BOOKS

Books which give an overview of modern Paganism are:

Margot Adler, *Drawing Down the Moon: Witches, Druids, Goddess-worshippers and other Pagans in America today*, Beacon Press, Boston, 1986. This is an excellent survey of North American Paganism with extensive lists of organizations and magazines, but some of the addresses are now out of date.

Vivianne Crowley, *Phoenix from the Flame: Living as a Pagan in the twenty-first century*, Thorsons, London, 1996, describes in more depth than is possible in this book the origins of the major Western Pagan traditions and the philosophy of Western Paganism.

Journalist Anthony Kemp has given a good overview of modern Witchcraft and Paganism in Britain in his hardback book *Witchcraft and Paganism Today*, Michael O'Mara Books, London, 1993.

An academic book which examines the philosophy of one aspect of Paganism – pantheism – is by philosopher/lecturer Michael P. Levine, who is based at the University of Western Australia: *Pantheism: A non-theistic concept of deity*, Routledge, London and New York, 1994. The book is somewhat frustrating in that it ignores modern day pantheists and focuses on those known to academic philosophers. However, it is useful for Pagans who need to articulate their beliefs in Interfaith and academic settings.

LARGE PAGAN ORGANIZATIONS/MAIN JOURNALS

UK and Europe

The Pagan Federation, BM Box 7097, London WC1N 3XX, UK; Fax: 01691 671066, is the main Pagan group in Europe. The Pagan Federation is a democratic organization run by its voting members. It has an annual conference in London, regional conferences, local group meetings and contacts world-wide. It publishes *Pagan Dawn*, an informative quarterly journal, and has a useful information pack on modern European Paganism and a Wicca information pack. Pagan books can be bought through mail order. Part

of the work of the Pagan Federation is to counter prejudice against Pagans and to provide accurate information on Paganism to government bodies, the media and the general public. The Pagan Federation administers the Pagan Prison Chaplaincy Service in the UK, is pleased to foster Interfaith contacts and can provide speakers for events.

North America

Circle, PO Box 219, Mount Horeb, WI 53572, USA, organizes Pagan events, fosters contacts and networking, and publishes *Circle Network News*, an informative journal of Nature Spirituality. Circle publishes *The Circle Guide to Pagan Groups* which lists groups in North America and can supply books by mail order. There are gatherings, a land sanctuary, counselling service and many other activities.

COMPUTER PAGANISM

Another way of contacting Pagans world-wide is via modem. Pagans are probably the most computer-literate spiritual community in the world. Contacts are available at the following addresses:

Church of All Worlds: listserv@netcom.com is an on-line Pagan congregation.

Pagan Computer BBS: Black Dog (UK) – 0181–983 3472.

Pagan Electronic Mail: to subscribe send a message to owner-uk-pagans@mono.city.ac.uk.

Newsgroups: alt. pagan

UK and Europe

Antaios, 168 rue Washington bte 2, B–1050 Bruxelles, Belgium, is a very interesting French-language magazine which has good articles on Classical Paganism.

Green Circle, PO Box 280, Maidstone ME16 0UL, UK, is a network of discussion groups in the UK and Europe established by Pagan writer Marian Green. *Green Circular* magazine can be purchased by members.

Hexenzeitschrift, Igor Warneck, Alterweg 8, D–57439 Attendorn, Germany, is a well-produced magazine for Nature religion and magic.

Hoblink, 'Out' Bookshop, 4–7 Dorset Street, Brighton BL2 1WA, UK, is an organization for gay and bisexual Pagans which produces a quarterly newsletter.

Irish Pagan Network, Bridge House, Clonegal, Enniscorthy, Ireland, organizes workshops, gatherings and seasonal rites. There is a quarterly newsletter *Pagan Life*.

Moira, CDD, BP 68, 33034 Bordeaux, France, is a Pagan and Wiccan magazine and contact point for French-language Wicca. Moira can provide home study training in French.

Norwegian Pagan Federation, PO Box 1814, Nordnes, 524 Bergen, Norway, is an information network for Scandinavian countries.

Pagan Animal Rights, c/o Billy Frugal, 10 Broughton St, Hebden Bridge, W. Yorks HX7 9JY, UK, works for the ethical treatment of animals and issues a magazine.

Pagan Hospice and Funeral Trust, BM Box 3337, London WC1N 3XX, UK, provides information on the spiritual and emotional aspects of dying, caring and death. There is a newsletter.

Talking Stick, PO Box 3719, London SW17 8XT, UK, is the high quality quarterly magazine of the Talking Stick esoteric discussion forum which meets fortnightly in a Central London pub. This is well worth a visit for visitors to London.

North America

Church of All Worlds, PO Box 212, Redwood Valley, California 95470, USA, is a Pagan organization which owns land, raises ecological awareness through its subsidiary organization, *Forever Forests*, and publishes the magazine *Green Egg*, PO Box 1542, Ukiah, CA 95482, USA. Gatherings are organized.

Earth Spirit Community, PO Box 365, Medford, Massachusetts 02155, USA, fosters Pagan networking in the mid-Atlantic area and runs workshops, talks and an annual festival.

International Gay and Lesbian Pagan Coalition, PO Box 26442, Oklahoma City, OK 73126–0442, USA, produces a newsletter and information pack and works against defamation.

Mid-West Pagan Council, PO Box 313, Matteson, Illinois 60442–0313, USA, is an association of Pagan groups in the Midwest which runs an annual Pagan Festival.

New Moon New York, PO Box 1471, Madison Square Station, New York 10159, USA, is a Pagan networking organization which runs open festivals and publishes *Our Pagan Times*.

Pagan Prisoners, PO Box 1510, Ellicott City, MD 21041, USA, runs a free newsletter for Pagan prison inmates.

Australia and New Zealand

Church of All Worlds, PO Box 408, Woden, ACT 2606, Australia, is the Australian branch of CAW.

Pan-Pacific Pagan Alliance, PO Box A486, Sydney South, NSW 2000, Australia, is the organization for all branches of Paganism in Australia and New Zealand. Its members' magazine lists groups and contacts and the PPPA can advise on Pagan matters generally.

Pan-Pacific Pagan Alliance, 516 Huon Road, South Hobart, Tasmania 7000.

Pan-Pacific Pagan Alliance, 21 Nelson Street, Helensville, New Zealand.

ECO-PAGANISM

BOOKS

An important academic book by a non-Pagan which nevertheless sets out many ideas which are found within the Pagan traditions is by biologist and Christian Rupert Sheldrake, *The Rebirth of Nature: The greening of science and God*, Century, London, 1990. This provides a fascinating overview of the origins of our ecological crisis and the implications of current scientific thinking for our relationship to Nature.

JOURNALS/ORGANIZATIONS

Dragon, 2 Sandford Walk, London SE14 6NB, UK, is a national network combining eco-magic with practical

conservation and campaigning. Events are organized across Britain. There is a newsletter, *Dragon Update*.

FAMILY PAGANISM

BOOKS

Two practical books for integrating Paganism into family life are:

Ashleen O'Gaea, *The Family Wicca Book: The Craft for parents and children*, Llewellyn, 1993;

Ceisiwir Serith, *The Pagan Family: Handing the old ways down*, Llewellyn, 1994;

and a useful British book for those creating seasonal celebrations is:

Marian Green, *A Calendar of Festivals: Traditional celebration, songs, seasonal recipes and things to make*, Element Books, Shaftesbury, UK, and Rockport, Mass., 1991.

JOURNALS

Magazines are beginning to appear for Pagan parents and children:

From the Heart, c/o K. Hinds, 2357 Loraine St NE, Atlanta, GA 30319, USA, is a newsletter for Pagan parents.

How About Magic (HAM), Nemeton, Box 488, Laytonville, CA 954 54, USA, is a magazine produced by Pagan children.

Toadstool, PO Box 428, Granville 2142, NSW, Australia, is a magazine and workbook for Pagan children aged 9–13 years.

BOOKS

The main Celtic myths available in English are those of Wales and Ireland:

The Welsh myth cycle is in the *Mabinogion* and contains much of the Welsh version of the Arthurian myth. This can be found in Jeffrey Gantz, trans., *The Mabinogion*, Penguin Books, Harmondsworth, 1976.

Irish myth cycles are more scattered. The Ulster myth cycles are found in:

T. Kinsella, *The Táin*, Dublin, 1969.
C. O'Rahilly, *Táin Bó Cuailnge*, Dublin, 1970.

Other material is found in:

P. McCana, *Celtic Mythology*, London, 1983.
T. P. Cross and C. H. Slover, *Ancient Irish Tales*, London, 1937.

A useful book on the Celtic traditions is Nora Chadwick, *The Celts*, Penguin Books, Harmondsworth, 1970.

Philip Carr-Gomm is the head of the Order of Bards, Ovates and Druids, which is the main Druid order in Europe. OBOD also has groves in the United States. He has written two books which give useful insights into Druidry:

Elements of The Druid Tradition, Element Books, 1991, describes the basics of modern Druidry.
The Druids's Way, Element Books, 1993, is the poetic and personal view of a practising Druid.

Caitlín and John Matthews are prolific writers on Celtic and Arthurian Tradition and are past Presiders of the

Order of Bards, Ovates and Druids. A basic introductory text which will give you a flavour of their work is Caitlín Matthews, *Elements of the Celtic Tradition*, Element Books, Shaftesbury, 1989.

JOURNALS/ORGANIZATIONS

UK and Europe

Celtic Research and Folklore Society, Spion Kop, Lamlash, Isle of Arran KA27, Scotland, publishes the useful journal *Seanchas* for those interested in Celtic Paganism.

Le Druidisme, c/o Pierre de la Crau, BP 13, 93301 Aubervillers Cedex, France, is an interesting French-language Druid magazine.

Druid's Voice, PO Box 29, St Leonard's on Sea, E. Sussex TN37 7YP, UK, is the twice-yearly journal of the *Council of British Druid Orders*, the umbrella organization for all Druid groups – Pagan, Christian and cultural – in Britain.

La Fédération Druidiques des Gaules, publishes a newsletter, *Combutis*, which is available from Pierre Collier, 8 rue P. Curie, 59195 Herin, France.

Order of Bards, Ovates and Druids, PO Box 1333, Lewes BN7 3ZG, UK, is the largest Druid order in Europe. OBOD offers training in Druidry covering healing, divination, mythology, history and folklore through correspondence courses, workshops and retreats in Europe and the United States. There is a members' magazine.

Ordos, 111 rue du Gl Buat, 44000 Nantes, France, is a journal of *mythes, mystères et légendes de la tradition celtique*.

Tuatha Ceatha, One World Centre, Canavan House, Nun's Island, Galway, Ireland, is a well-produced magazine of Native Irish spirituality with listings of events and contacts.

North America

Ar nDraiocht Fein, PO Box 9420, Newark DE 19714–9420, USA, is the largest Druid organization in North America. ADF practises Neo-Pagan Druidism, has a journal *The Druid's Progress* and offers training in Druidry.

Keltria, PO Box 33284, Minneapolis, MN 55433, USA, broke away from Ar nDraiocht Fein a few years ago to focus more specifically on Celtic Druidry as opposed to ADF's eclectic use of Indo-European sources. Keltria runs a Druid training course through correspondence and a magazine.

WICCA AND WISECRAFT

BOOKS

Vivianne Crowley, *Wicca: The old religion in the new millennium*, Thorsons, 1995, explores Wicca as a initiatory Mystery Tradition for men and women. For non-English speakers, the first edition is available in Dutch as *Hekserij: Een oude leer voor de nieuwe tijd*, Elsy Kloeg, trans., Kosmos, Utrecht, and in German as *Wicca: Die alte Religion im neuen Zeitalter*, Michael de Witt, trans., Edition Ananael, Wien, Austria.

The ideas contained in the book form part of a workshop and correspondence teaching course through the *Wicca Study Group*, BM Deosil, London WC1N 3XX, UK, which is the main teaching organization for Wicca in Europe. This is co-ordinated by Vivianne and Chris Crowley and other tutors. The WSG provides teaching on Wicca and WiseCraft for group and solo paths through workshops and a 12–18 month home study course. The course is available in English, French and German. The WSG functions mainly in Europe but workshops can be arranged in other parts of the world by request.

Two very good books on solo WiseCraft in the British tradition are:

Rae Beth, *Hedgewitch: A guide to the solitary practitioner*, Hale, 1990;
Marian Green, *A Witch Alone*, Thorsons, London, 1996.

JOURNALS/ORGANIZATIONS

UK and Europe

Cauldron, available from Mike Howard, Caemorgan Cottage, Caemorgan Road, Cardigan, Dyfed SA43 1QU, UK, is an informative journal of the Old Religion.

Circe, Postbus 2191, 3500 GD Utrecht, The Netherlands, provides Wiccan contacts in the Netherlands and Craft supplies.

Coraen, Moonsstraat 11, 2018 Antwerpen, Belgium, is a teaching coven in Belgium. Contact can also be provided to Craft in the Netherlands.

Hole in the Sky, Postlargernd, D–13507 Berlin 27, Germany, provides information on German-speaking Wicca, Wiccan activities and workshops.

Marian Green publishes the magazine *Quest*, BCM–SCL Quest, London WC1N 3XX, UK, which is one of the oldest Craft magazines. *Quest* has its own annual conference.

Marian Green also runs a teaching organization, the *Invisible College*, which can be contacted at the *Quest* address. The Invisible College teaches natural magic and the solo Craft through correspondence courses and workshops in the UK and Europe.

Wiccan Rede, PO Box 473, Zeist, NL 3700 AL, The Netherlands, is an English/Dutch Wiccan magazine which can assist with contacts in the Netherlands.

North America

Aquarian Tabernacle Church, PO Box 73, Index, Washington 98256, USA, is a Wiccan church which provides teaching in Paganism and is active in Interfaith work. There are ATC affiliated organizations in Australia.

Covenant of the Goddess, PO Box 1226, Berkeley, CA 94704, USA, is a federation of Wiccan covens which publishes a newsletter and holds an annual gathering.

Hecate's Loom, Box 5206, Station B, Victoria, BC, V8R 6N4, Canada, is one of the largest and oldest Pagan publications in Canada. It focuses on West coast Wiccan activities.

Wic-can Fest, PO Box 125, 3090 Danforth Avenue, Scarboro, Ontario, M1L 1B1, Canada, is a open festival which takes place every year near Toronto.

Wiccan Church of Canada, 109 Vaughan Road, Toronto, M6C 2L9, Canada, is a network of Wiccan groups in the Odyssian tradition. It offers training, information and ritual celebrations and publishes a magazine, *The Chalice and the Blade*.

Web of Wyrd, PO Box A486, Sydney South, NSW 2000, Australia, is an informative Wiccan and Pagan magazine.

NORTHERN TRADITION

BOOKS

The Northern Tradition myths are found in the *Eddas*. There are two versions which are important: the *Prose Edda*, which tells the stories of the Gods, and the *Poetic Edda*, which renders these into beautiful verse. To gain an understanding of the power and beauty of the Northern Tradition, it is necessary to read both. The *Prose Edda* can be found in:

Snorri Sturloson, *Edda*, Anthony Faulkes, trans., Everyman Library, J.M. Dent, London, 1987.

The *Poetic Edda* can be found in:

W. H. Auden and Paul B. Taylor, eds., *Norse Poems*, Faber and Faber, 1983.

Lee M. Hollander, trans., *The Poetic Edda*, University of Texas Press, Austin, Texas, 1962.

Neither translation is entirely satisfactory. The Auden translation has better poetry, but there are distortions in the text which reflect the preconceptions of the translators, such as changing the sex of the Moon from male to female. The Hollander translation, on the other hand, does not convey the beauty of the poetry or that the *Eddas* form part of an oral skaldic tradition.

Some of the best translations are found in the work of a writer of Northern European origin: Elsa-Brita Titchenell, *The Masks of Odin: Wisdom of the Ancient Norse*, Theosophical University Press, Pasadena, California, 1985. This is a beautiful and inspiring book with translations and interpretations of the principal poems of the Northern Tradition.

Another insightful book which relates the Northern Tradition to other Pagan traditions such as Wicca is Freya Aswynn, *Leaves of Yggdrasil: A Synthesis of Magic, Feminine Mysteries, Folklore*, Llewellyn, 1990.

A prominent academic, Hilda Ellis Davidson, has done valuable work comparing Northern and Celtic traditions. All her books are highly readable and can be recommended:

Hilda R. Ellis Davidson, *Gods and Myths of Northern Europe*, Pelican, Harmondsworth, 1964;
Scandinavian Mythology, Hamlyn, 1982;
Myths and Symbols in Pagan Europe: Early Scandinavian and Celtic religions, Manchester University Press, 1988.

JOURNALS/ORGANIZATIONS

UK and Europe

Dorn, c/o F. Thierart, Poste Restante, Reims Ceres, 51084 Reims Cedex, France, is a French-language magazine for the Northern Tradition.

Odinshof, BCM Tercel, London WC1N 3XX, UK, is a registered religious charity for those worshipping the Norse Gods. It offers contact with groups and a correspondence course. The Odinshof runs a land guardian scheme which

purchases woodland for Pagan conservation. Donations for the land scheme are welcome.

Odinic Rite is a registered charity offering guidance for those seeking the Northern path. The OR publishes a magazine and informative guides on setting up groups and conducting rites. There are two branches of the Odinic Rite with different magazines. Their addresses are: BM Edda or BM Runic, London WC1N 3XX, UK.

Odinic Rite – France, *Hearth d'Irmin*, BP 21–46, F–51081 Reims Cedex, publishes the newsletter *La Lettre d'Irmin* and provides information on the Northern Tradition in France.

North America

Arizona Kindred, PO Box 961, Payson, Arizona 85547, USA, is a large Northern Tradition group which publishes a magazine, *Odin's Folk*.

Asatru Free Assembly, PO Box 1754, Breckenbridge, Texas 76024, USA, works to promote Scandinavian/German Paganism through its networking, a magazine, *The Runestone*, and an annual festival, the Althing.

Wyrd Network, PO Box 970, Amherst, MA 01004, USA, works to bridge the gap between Wicca and Asatru and to incorporate Norse deities into Wicca.

Yggdrasil, 537 Jones St #165, San Francisco, CA 94102, USA, is published by Freya's Folk, and is a quarterly journal of Pagan culture.

NATIVE AMERICAN TRADITION AND SHAMANISM

BOOKS

Recommending books on the Native American traditions is somewhat sensitive. Not all Native American tribes appreciate the way their cultural and spiritual heritage has been hijacked by money-making Westerners. The wisdom of Native American Paganism can, however, be very illuminating to those of us whose Pagan heritage is more distant and who are striving to rebuild our Pagan spirituality. Books which take a useful, but Western-centred approach are:

Michael Harner, *The Way of the Shaman*, Harper & Row, New York, 1980;

Kenneth Meadows, *The Medicine Way*, Element Books, Shaftesbury, 1990.

Those wishing to understand Native American culture on a deeper level are recommended to read books on particular tribal cultures. It should not be assumed that Native American spirituality has a single framework and spirituality cannot be divorced from its tribal social context. Native American spirituality is a number of complex and divergent traditions.

The spiritual view of the Native Americans of the Plains is conveyed in the life story of the Oglala Lakota Holy Man Black Elk. Black Elk was born in 1863 and his story was recorded in the early 1930s when he was an old man and had seen the traumatic and terrible history of his people unfold. He wanted to ensure that his spiritual vision should not be lost and so allowed the poet John Neihardt to write it down: John G. Neihardt, *Black Elk Speaks*, University of Nebraska Press, 1979.

Another interesting book on the mythology of a very different people, the Hopi of the South West, is Frank Waters, *The Book of the Hopi: The first revelation of the Hopis' historical and religious worldview of life*, Penguin Books, NY. Like Black Elk's vision, Hopi spirituality has important messages for the modern world.

JOURNALS/ORGANIZATIONS

Some organizations and magazines for those interested in Native American spirituality and Shamanism are:

UK and Europe

Pathways, 28 Cowl Street, Evesham, Worcestershire WR11 4PL, UK, runs courses on contemporary Shamanism and on skills such as drum-making. Pathways produces the magazine *Sacred Hoop* which focuses on Native American spirituality.

North America

Foundation for Shamanic Studies, PO Box 670, Norwalk, Connecticut 06852, USA, is a non-profit making educational organization which teaches Shamanic techniques based on the work of Michael Harner. There is a quarterly newsletter for members.

Shaman's Drum: A Journal of Experiential Shamanism, PO Box 430, Willits, CA 95490, USA, is a high quality and fascinating journal of experiential shamanism published by the Cross-Cultural Shamanism Network which contains useful articles and resource listings. It also focuses on issues threatening indigenous peoples and the planet as a whole.

There is a readers' subscription sponsorship scheme for prisoners and senior citizens.

BALTIC AND FINNISH PAGANISM

The Baltic countries of Europe – Lithuania, Latvia and Estonia – were the last to be Christianized. Lithuania did not become Christian until the fifteenth century and Paganism has been preserved there in greater entirety than in other parts of the Western world. Baltic Paganism is a flourishing movement which has fostered cultural renewal. Its members were persecuted under the Soviets.

BOOKS

Feminist academic Marija Gimbutas, who was herself of Lithuanian origin, wrote some fascinating books on Baltic and Slavic Paganism:

The Slavs, Thames and Hudson, 1971;

The Balts, Thames and Hudson, 1963.

JOURNALS/ORGANIZATIONS

UK and Europe

Starlight, PO Box 452, 00101 Helsinki, Finland, provides information on the Paganism and Wicca in Finland.

North America

There are organizations in North America for those interested in Baltic spirituality. These can provide contact with groups in Europe.

Romuva Canada, PO Box 232, Station 'D', 4975 Dundas St West, Etobicoke, Ontario, M9A 4X2, Canada.

Romuva USA, PO Box 214, Athens, OH 45701, USA, publishes the English language journal of the *Lithuanian Ethnic Church Romuva of the USA Inc.* which can advise on all aspects of Lithuanian Paganism.

PAGANISM FOR WOMEN AND MEN

Paganism is a revival of ancient religious traditions, but it is concerned with the realities of life today. Male–female relations and the balance of energy between Goddess and God are the concern of many who are drawn to Paganism. Some of these issues have been addressed in books which are specifically Pagan. Other useful books have been written by those working in men's and women's groups, politics and humanistic and transpersonal psychology.

GODDESS PAGANISM

BOOKS

An important book on feminist religion is Z. Budapest, *The Holy Book of Women's Mysteries*, Harper and Row, 1990.

A classic text on the Goddess is Monica Sjöö and Barbara Mor, *The Great Cosmic Mother*, Harper and Row, 1981.

The American feminist Witch Starhawk's book has gone through two editions and will no doubt continue to be a classical of feminist WiseCraft for many years to come. Her work is important for both women and men. Starhawk, *The Spiral Dance: A rebirth of the ancient religion of the Great Goddess*, Harper and Row, San Francisco, 1989 edition.

UK and Europe

Fellowship of Isis, Clonegal Castle, Clonegal, Enniscorthy, Ireland, is a world-wide Goddess organization, many of whose members belong to other Pagan groups and organizations. Some of its members run *Iseums*, Goddess groups, which meet regularly. There is provision for training in the priesthood. In recent years the FOI has established an annual conference in London. It publishes *Isian News*. The FOI also runs the *Druid Clan of Dana* which has its own magazine, *Aisling*, available from PO Box 196, London WC1N 3XX, UK. The *Fellowship of Isis* itself is run from the home of the Hon. Olivia Durdin-Robertson.

North America

Reclaiming, PO Box 14404, San Francisco, California 94114, USA, is a Center for Feminist Spirituality – a collective of women and men working to unify spirituality and politics. It offers workshops, summer programmes, public rituals, a newsletter and is inspired by work of Starhawk.

SageWoman, PO Box 641, Point Arena, CA 95468–0641, USA, is a quarterly magazine of women's spirituality, celebrating the Goddess in every woman.

MEN'S PAGANISM

BOOKS

An important book for men is that of the Jungian therapist Joseph Campbell. This explores issues of the modern male life cycle through heroic Pagan myths: Joseph Campbell, *The Hero with a Thousand Faces*, Bollingen Series XVII, Princeton University Press, 1972.

Another book which takes a psychotherapeutic approach but which examines modern Paganism and in particular Wicca is the book by English psychologist John Rowan, *The Horned God: Feminism and men as wounding and healing*, Routledge & Kegan Paul, London, 1987.

Other Pagan-oriented books are:

John Matthews, *Choirs of the God: Revisioning masculinity*, Mandala, London, 1991;
R. J. Stewart, *Celebrating the Male Mysteries*, Arcania, Bath, 1991.

JOURNALS/ORGANIZATIONS

UK and Europe

Everyman, PO Box 459, Oxford OX2 2YH, UK, runs workshops for men and publishes *Passages: A journal of gender, earth and soul.*

North America

Wingspan, Box 1491, Manchester, Maine 01944, USA, is a journal of the male spirit.

Of further interest...

PRINCIPLES OF NLP

THE ONLY INTRODUCTION YOU'LL EVER NEED

Joseph O'Connor and Ian McDermott

Neuro-Linguistic Programming (NLP) is the psychology of excellence. It is based on the practical skills that are used by all good communicators to obtain excellent results. These skills are invaluable for personal and professional development. This introductory guide explains:

- what NLP is
- how to use it in your life personally, spiritually and professionally
- how to understand body language
- how to achieve excellence in everything that you do

Joseph O'Connor is a trainer, consultant and software designer. He is the author of the bestselling *Introducing NLP* and several other titles, including *Successful Selling with NLP* and *Training with NLP.*

Ian McDermott is a certified trainer with the Society of Neuro-Linguistic Programming. He is the Director of Training for International Teaching Seminars, the leading NLP training organization in the UK.

PRINCIPLES OF THE ENNEAGRAM

Karen Webb

There is a growing fascination with the Enneagram – the ancient uncannily accurate model of personality types linking personality to spirit. Most people can recognize themselves as one of the nine archetypes. This introduction to the subject explains:

- the characteristics of the nine types
- how the system works
- ways of understanding your own personality
- how to discover your true potential and attain it
- ways to enhance your relationships

Karen Webb is an experienced Enneagram teacher, counsellor and workshop leader. She has introduced many people to the system and guided them in using the information to change their lives. She has been employed by many large companies as a management consultant.

PRINCIPLES OF TAROT

Evelyne and Terry Donaldson

Tarot has fascinated people for hundreds of years, but at times the symbolism can be difficult to relate to our contemporary lives. This introductory guide demystifies the tarot and clearly explains:

- the meaning of each card
- how to do a reading for yourself and other people
- how to use the tarot as a tool for personal development
- easy ways of gaining a deeper understanding of this ancient art

Evelyne and Terry Donaldson are highly experienced tarot teachers and readers. They run the London Tarot Training Centre. Terry Donaldson is the author of *Step by Step Tarot*, also published by Thorsons, co-creator of the *Dragon Tarot* deck and *Wyvern, the game of Dragons, Dragon-Slayers and Treasure.*

PRINCIPLES OF NLP	0 7225 3195 8	£5.99
PRINCIPLES OF THE ENNEAGRAM	0 7225 30191 5	£5.99
PRINCIPLES OF TAROT	0 7225 3217 2	£5.99
PRINCIPLES OF HYPNOTHERAPY	0 7225 3242 3	£5.99
PRINCIPLES OF SELF-HEALING	1 85538 486 8	£5.99
PRINCIPLES OF COLONIC IRRIGATION	0 7225 3029 3	£5.99
PRINCIPLES OF AROMATHERAPY	0 7225 3263 6	£5.99

All these books are available from your local bookseller or can be ordered direct from the publishers.

To order direct just tick the titles you want and fill in the form below:

Name: ______________________________
Address: ______________________________
____
Postcode: ______________________________

Send to Thorsons Mail Order, Dept 3, HarperCollinsPublishers, Westerhill Road, Bishopbriggs, Glasgow G64 2QT.

Please enclose a cheque or postal order or your authority to debit your Visa/Access account —

Credit card no: ______________________________
Expiry date: ______________________________
Signature: ______________________________

— up to the value of the cover price plus:
UK & BFPO: Add £1.00 for the first book and 25p for each additional book ordered.

Overseas orders including Eire: Please add £2.95 service charge. Books will be sent by surface mail but quotes for airmail dispatches will be given on request.

24-HOUR TELEPHONE ORDERING SERVICE FOR ACCESS/VISA CARD-HOLDERS — TEL: 0141 772 2281.